# The Complete Guide to Quick and Easy Marketing that Works

## by David N Russell

*"In the past two weeks since I read your book we have had free press coverage with more to follow. Due to the PR several people attended the exhibition especially to visit our stand. The extra business was much appreciated. If that wasn't enough, we also won the best stand award (out of 200 stands) at our very first show. All this has been achieved by following your step by step, tried and tested advice. Thank you"* — *Martin Higgs, QRS Cleaning*

"Since putting some of the ideas in the book into effect, we have reduced the cost of our advertising by 20%. And we haven't yet taken steps to make the advertising more effective or to increase the response rate, or tried out all the other ideas in the book, but when we do..." — *David Burch, Music Monsters*

*"I bought the book via mail order, thinking that I could keep it for the allowed time and then send it back if necessary... Wild Horses wouldn't drag it away from me mow! I've found it particularly useful for exhibitions – we always stand out now."* — Jane Wyles, Hickling & Squires Ltd

"Congratulations on a fantastic book. You have certainly taken the mystique out of marketing" — *Mike Le Put, MLP Training*

The Complete Guide to Quick and Easy Marketing that Works
Copyright ©1995 David N Russell

Published by Marketing Matters, 2 Butlin Close, Rothwell, Northants NN14 6YA. Tel. 01536 710050

ISBN Number 0-9525508-0-6

First printed April 1995. Re-printed December 1995, January 1997, January 1999

Illustrations by Ken Verow (Tel. 01933 276108)

# The Complete Guide to Quick and Easy Marketing that Works

## by David N Russell

*To Kelly, Pamela, Mum and Dad*

# Preface

If you are involved in marketing, the chances are that you will be asked "what's it all about?" on a fairly frequent basis. **"Marketing"** seems to be a subject that most people have a vague idea about, but not many understand to any great extent. In many cases explanations are considerably overcomplicated - *but, don't worry, that's not the case here.*

When I attended my very first marketing lecture at college I was terribly relieved. It was the first time in twelve months that I had sat through two hours of new information and actually understood most of it quite clearly. It seemed simple. It seemed common sense.

Later, inevitably, it all got a touch more complicated - after all, you have to be able to prove that you can wrestle with the most complex of problems if you want to earn yourself a proper qualification - don't you? Not surprisingly, I didn't seem to use too much of the complicated theory in my first "marketing" jobs - just the common sense.

Since college I have often been asked by colleagues, employees and friends to lend books on "marketing" to help with courses or work. I have found myself saying "You can take a look through these, but I doubt whether you'll find much of relevance". The problem seemed to be that books provided the facts and the theory, but not much in the way of practical answers. *They were just too heavyweight.*

So, after 15 years of using common sense marketing techniques reasonably successfully, I decided to set about writing a marketing book of my own which could be used as quickly as it could be read. A book that would give clear, simple guidance providing a foundation for other, more substantial plans. **In short, a book that would make sense and make things happen** - a book to generate more customers quickly if that was what was needed.

I have been lucky enough to have worked in organisations where I have been able to try new things, to take chances and to develop new ideas. I am grateful for that. My thanks go to my "unique" boss, Sten, for the support and freedom throughout the years. Without that freedom to test and to try I doubt whether I would have gained so much knowledge and experience. Many other people have helped too, both in the production of this book and throughout the past few years. My gratitude goes to Sheila, Bob & Sue, Steve, John C, Alastair & Carole, Bob at Direct, Julian, John Mac, and Tina for their advice, comments and inspiration.

I hope that you will enjoy reading the book, because if you enjoy reading it then the chances are that you will understand it and learn from it. Whatever you are hoping to do with the ideas and the knowledge, I wish you all the success possible.

**David N Russell**

# Introduction

**Congratulations.** You have in your hands information that could make your business more effective and more successful. What a bargain! For just a few pounds you have gained over **_One Million Pounds worth_** of marketing advice. That's how much I reckon I've spent on various projects over the past 15 years or so. Some have worked well, some not so well, but whatever the outcome you can learn from the experience simply by spending a few hours reading the book.

_Fifteen years of experience crammed into just 100 or so pages._

Throughout the pages of this book you will find ideas that will both save you money and help you to develop the awareness and the profile of your company and, as a result, increase your sales.

**_That's the good news._** The bad news is that just reading this book isn't going to make your business more successful. Like most good things in life you will have to put some effort into making the most of the ideas you'll find. If you are a person of action - great, but if you need to be pushed into action, then for goodness sake find someone to push you, because you'll get little from the hundreds of ideas in this book unless you are willing to try them.

The book is made up of sections relating to all the major elements of marketing activity - Advertising, Public Relations, Exhibitions and Direct Mail. The majority of my work over the years has fallen into one of these categories and so I am confident that the book will provide both useful and functional advice for anyone wishing to broaden the promotional activities of their own company or organisation. The final section is about becoming the best and is a more general look at how you can be one step ahead of the competition. Each of the sections have a number of separate chapters, taking you through the subject in what I hope will prove to be an organised manner.

Now that you have made the decision to spend some of your hard earned money on a book about marketing, it would be a shame if you didn't use some of the ideas to make sure you got the most out of it now wouldn't it?

_So, with an open mind, let's begin ..._

# Contents

# What is marketing anyway?

"Marketing." It means so many different things to so many different people. You'll find endless definitions within the hundreds of marketing books in the library.

I would rather keep it as simple as possible. For myself, marketing can best be summed up as **"making things happen"**. Enabling businesses to succeed.

Of course, "making things happen" covers a huge range of activities. However, whether it is increasing awareness of a new product through an advertising campaign, launching a new service locally, building relationships with key suppliers or even making sure that your telephones are answered properly, then you are making things happen in a positive way. You are practising "marketing".

Simple isn't it? And it is. In fact, it's so simple that most organisations are marketing themselves already - even if they don't think that they are. All of us are marketing ourselves each and every day, even if it's just the way we talk to the boss to get an agreement to leave 10 minutes early.

The aim of this book is to give a lead and the encouragement to try a few simple promotional ideas. I realise that most smaller organisations just don't have either the spare cash or time to endlessly research methods and options before they take action. They need a simple approach which they can easily understand.

## SO WHAT'S SO DIFFERENT ABOUT THESE IDEAS? ...

*Good question.* What makes the ideas you are about to read so different? Aren't they just another set of principles and theories from yet another "Consultant" who believes that he knows the right way forward?

Not quite.

For the most part, my book is based on ideas that I have used or have been used by one of my colleagues or competitors and that have been effective. There's very little theory here - just practical ideas that you can implement as soon as you put the book down if you wish.

*It seems to me that many marketing books are just too complicated.* After the first few pages they seem to assume that we are a chairman of a major corporation. In contrast, this book is full of very simple, very easy to implement, common sense ideas which you can use quickly to get a result. **In other words, ideas which can help to make the 'phones ring, pull customers through the door or generate enquiries whichever way you wish.**

I have no problem using ideas that my competitors have used. Generally there are very few absolutely new ideas around in the marketing world. Whatever idea you have, the chances are that someone, somewhere will have used it before and either made it a great success or found it to be a flop. New ideas are few and far between and so you shouldn't be shy when it comes to taking an idea that appeals and adapting it to work for yourself. After all, there's no need to invent the wheel every time.

One of my most important working files is my **"Snatch File"**. My snatch file is where I keep all the ideas I really like for a rainy day when I may be struggling to create something new myself. Think about it. Very few smaller businesses can afford to employ the talents of really effective creative people. However, you can still enjoy their input. You'll see their work on show in all the national newspapers and magazines.

If an idea for an advertisement catches your eye, cut it out and place it in your snatch file. When a headline really attracts you, make a note of it for your next campaign. Even if you don't action one of the promotional ideas in this book, make yourself a file, right now, that you can fill with creative work that appeals. Before long you'll have thousands of pounds worth of creative ideas at your fingertips, ready to be adapted for your own use, just when you are ready to use them.

Throughout this book you will find **"Action Points"**. These are simple little tasks which you can complete quickly. To get the most out of these action points, complete them as soon as you read them. If you don't, then you'll forget to do them and will have lost an opportunity.

## DON'T TRUST YOUR MEMORY...

Don't waste your thoughts by not getting them down on paper when you first think of them. If you need to, scribble all over this book while you are reading it. This book isn't meant to sit on your bookshelf for years to come gathering dust so don't worry about defacing it.

If one of my ideas triggers off an idea of your own - **get it down on paper fast.** Even if after your initial thought you decide that your idea is a little off the mark, don't worry. Get it down so that you can read it time and time again and almost certainly it will trigger another idea that you will be able to use with some success. Ideas are far too valuable to discount, however crazy they may seem at first, so store them up and keep going back to them.

I tend to use a magic marker to highlight the parts of a book that I am really interested in. That way I can review the book every few months if I need to, just by flicking through and concentrating on the words, sentences or paragraphs that I have highlighted. I have found this to be a really useful method - maybe you will too.

## WHAT MAKES ME SO SURE I'M RIGHT...

The information in this book has worked - but it might not work for you. Unfortunately there are no racing certainties in marketing. It's a case of finding out what's best for you. Anyone looking for a simple fix to make everything wonderful overnight may be disappointed.

Not everything in the book will suit you, but some things most certainly will and these are the ones to highlight, to think about and to adapt for your own use … maybe sooner rather than later.

*I can promise you that you'll be able to understand the ideas.* I know that because, for the most part, they are really simple. I have spent the majority of my business life in companies with limited marketing budgets and so I have been used to working with and developing simple, low cost methods of getting the message across. If you are under any misapprehensions that you have to be highly intelligent or that you need vast budgets to be able to market yourself or your company properly, then think again … you don't.

## HOLD ON TO YOUR HATS, HERE WE GO!

If you have bought this book it would seem to be a waste to not read on and discover for yourself if there's anything in the book that is worth the money. I know that there is. **In fact, there are ideas on most pages. So, don't stop turning the pages!**

*SECTION ONE*

# Advertising

*CHAPTER 1*

# The first steps to an effective advertising campaign

As they sort through the mounting number of invoices received from various magazines and newspapers and now on their desks waiting for payment, there must be thousands of businessmen who are wondering whether their advertising is actually producing results.

Although there's no doubt that advertising generally works, all the elements of a campaign need to be spot-on for the best results to be achieved. Many businesses needlessly waste resources because they make simple mistakes with their advertising or don't find enough time to do the job properly. Considering how expensive advertising can be, *it's amazing just how little attention some plans are given.*

It's all too easy to leave the advertising decisions to someone else. Someone like the smart, young, eager newspaper advertising representative only six weeks into the job. Surely they know what they are doing and can advise you on the best way to spend your money - can't they?

**It may not be the case.** The fact is that although they may be well versed on the benefits of their own product - the newspaper - they may not be quite as familiar with your product or service. It is unlikely that the advertising salesperson will know your business well enough for you to be able to let them get on with it without your input, - and really understanding your business is the first vital step to getting your advertising right.

In too many cases advertisers haven't really thought through exactly what sells their products before spending substantial amounts attempting to attract new customers with a message that may be off target. How then can you make sure that you've got at least a fighting chance of producing results when you decide to advertise for the first time? I hope that the next few pages will give you a few ideas to help make your promotions more effective all round.

## IS ADVERTISING RIGHT FOR YOU AT ALL?

Some companies advertising in your local press or your trade magazine might just as well be throwing their money down the drain - at least it would take less administration! It isn't always the case that every product is suitable for advertising. Sometimes other more cost-effective methods could be employed such as direct mail or maybe public relations. The first step therefore must be to decide whether advertising is right for your product or service and, if so, what type of advertising will produce the best results.

Why should some products be unsuitable for advertising? Surely anything can be promoted in the pages of a paper or magazine?

*Indeed they can, but with very different results.* It's important to understand your product or service appeal, but it's just as important to understand your market too. You need to be comfortable in the knowledge that you understand how your customers are generated and how to find more of the same. We have two critical components, the product and the market.

## AN EXAMPLE...

If you were selling office supplies in a small town, one option would be to use the local press to attract new business. However, if you think about it carefully, how many potential customers would you have in your area? If you estimate 1,000 businesses are potential customers and the newspaper is delivered to 50,000 homes in the area, then you are "talking" to 48,000 people who would never dream of buying a product from you. Maybe a letter and information pack sent directly to the 2,000 businesses would be more effective and more profitable. *It's all about targeting your customers in the best way.*

## LESSON ONE, TARGETING CUSTOMERS ...

Let's now assume that you own a video rental shop in a small town of only 5,000 people. Your market is made up of people living within the local community. Unless you are an exceptional video store or maybe part of a large national chain, the chances are that you aren't going to get very many customers travelling more than a few miles to buy from you. If they travel further they will probably have passed two or three other very similar video stores on their way. Clearly your market is in a very tightly defined geographical area. It is an easily defined **"TARGET MARKET"**.

Of course there are always exceptions. Some businesses are just so good at attracting and keeping their customers that their loyal contacts will travel some way to buy from them, passing similar outlets that could have sold them the same product, *sometimes at a cheaper price!* Companies that enjoy this type of loyalty don't just find that it happens. They work hard at creating a special relationship with their customers. We will be examining the methods used to build powerful and profitable customer loyalty later on.

Back at our video store and assuming that we haven't yet reached the stage where we can attract customers on a regular basis from further afield, you have the choice between a local newspaper being delivered to 25,000 homes and a regional paper that covers a much larger area, being circulated to over 85,000 homes. Based on what we know about our customer type, it would be sensible to choose the smaller paper as the wastage would be so much less. There may be other considerations of course, such as a special deal which is just too good to turn down, but generally the more local title would prove to be more cost-effective.

You should be able to spot the companies blasting away, promoting themselves to thousands of people who will never be in the market for their products. They may be better targeting their potential market more closely and reducing the wastage.

**Wastage - it's a horrible word.** Unfortunately the truth is that there is always going to be some wastage wherever you choose to advertise. There will always be readers who would never buy your product, no matter how hard you tried to sell to them. The trick is to ensure that your wastage is as little as possible. Understanding that your target market may be limited should encourage you to try to pinpoint where it is before committing funds.

*CHAPTER 2*
# Choosing the right place to advertise

If you are comfortable with the idea that your product will generate business through advertising, then how do you decide where to advertise?

If you are *"targeting"* your product very locally, then you may have a limited choice of newspapers or magazines. The first simple step is to take a look at your competitors, if you have any, and learn from them. After all, you don't want to re-invent the wheel if someone else has done the work and spent the money researching already. If a company you would consider to be your competitor, or a company that you feel may be trying to attract similar customers to your own is advertising in the same place time and time again you would assume that it would be working for them.

By following them into the media that they have chosen, you are automatically *"targeting"* your products correctly - unless of course they haven't a clue if their advertising is working at all, *when you will be taking just as much of a risk as they are!!*

At some stage, you will be contacted by an advertising representative from a newspaper or magazine - it may have already happened. At meetings they will have talked about circulation, readership, cost per square column centimetre and such like. What they probably will not have talked about is your business. In fact, in some cases the representative will not even know what type of business you are running when they first contact you.

*Action Point*
Before you consider spending on advertising, take time to think about your target market. Who are your customers? Where do they come from? What do they read? If you don't seem to get the time to "think" about these important points during a normal daytime, create an afternoon of "thinking time". Leave the office or home if you have too - but make sure that you give yourself some time to consider just who you should be targeting in the future.

## Action Point

Don't be confused between figures quoted for readership and circulation. Papers like to quote a bigger "readership" figure. This is the number of people that they estimate read the paper. However, in most cases, the circulation is the more important figure to bear in mind. That is, how many copies are either bought or given away.

## Quick Tip

If you are thinking of advertising for the very first time, and know which paper or magazine to use, ask for the Advertising Manager when you first call for information. In the same way that you would rather talk to a Solicitor than a Clerk if you have a legal problem, you should try to get the best free advice that you can. You probably will not be handled by the Manager on a day to day basis, but he or she is bound to have more experience than the representative who will eventually handle your account - so why not use it?

You will be able to tell how good they are at their jobs by the amount of knowledge they have of your needs. It is important that they understand something of your business, so that they are able to advise you in the future.

The very best advertising salespeople and the ones who stay in the job for some time, eventually earning promotion, know that it is pointless to encourage businesses to spend large amounts on advertising when no really serious consideration has been given to the objectives of the campaign. They also realise that if they spend a little time learning about your requirements and get it right, they are more likely to secure a client for many years to come. A client who will spend regularly.

Good advertising salespeople appreciate that each client is different and may need individual treatment in the way that advertising is prepared and displayed. If you feel that the representative who contacts you isn't in it for the longer term and is treating you as just another client, the alarm bells should be sounding. You could be in danger of losing control and losing money. You may be spending what is, for your business, a considerable amount and you deserve to get the best advice possible.

Generally advertising space is sold by younger people. It is often one of their first jobs (*it was my first job*). Because of this, some of them will tend to have limited experience of marketing in general or advertising in particular. You must be strong and not be sold to - at least until you are ready to buy. Later we will be covering how to buy advertising space effectively, so that you are in control and spending exactly what you want to spend.

To be certain that you are receiving the correct information to make your decision, ask more specific questions about companies who may already be using the paper - even your competitors. **You'd be surprised how much free market research information you can glean by talking to an eager advertising sales representative determined to secure your business.** If you need convincing further don't be shy to ask to see testimonials from companies that you sense may be selling to a similar type of customer. Even better, ask for a contact or two from non-competing companies to ring and hear their views of the paper and the results they have experienced.

*You may feel that these steps seem a little over-cautious.* After all, we are only talking about a small advertisement aren't we? Well, yes, you could view it that way. However, I prefer to see it as a method of preventing businesses losing thousands of pounds over a longer period when they are using the wrong media or wrong advertisement.

One small advertisement can lead to a six week run which, in turn, can lead to a six month promotional spell - all of which is proving far from effective. Building up a campaign this way is the easiest thing in the world as repeating advertising week after week is so simple to do. **Many businesses simply react to advertising offers week after week without ever performing any analysis to see if the budget is being spent wisely.**

Getting to know other businessmen and women and sharing ideas is a great way to learn quickly what might work and what may not, especially on a very local level. Joining a local business club is a good forum to swop experiences, especially if the businesses include those similar to your own in terms of size or progress. You might like to take a friend or a colleague along if you have a chat with another businessman, as sometimes it can be difficult to remember all the points raised if you are on your own and as they may be important, you will not want to forget them.

Another simple way of researching possible publications is to analyse the type of businesses using the paper or magazine, especially the larger companies who may be spending much larger amounts. The large national chains will most certainly have completed detailed research into their choice and will be using each individual title for a good reason.

If you have two papers to choose from and one carries far more advertising from national companies, then the chances are that the one promoting the national companies has more going for it in terms of effectiveness. Just as you can use the creative input worth thousands of pounds with a snatch file you can also acquire the benefit of costly media research courtesy of major companies - *just by using your own eyes.*

Bear in mind however, the point we made earlier about promoting to a wider audience than necessary. Most major companies will be looking to achieve a wider coverage and that may not be your first priority.

## AS THEY SAY, IT'S GOOD TO TALK ...

There is one group of people who can help a great deal in your media choice - and the good news is that for most companies they are quite easy to find.

**They are customers.**

These days *"customer profiling"* is becoming very popular. You may yourself have completed a questionnaire requesting details of lifestyle, preferences for various foods, sports, hobbies and papers bought. These surveys are used by larger companies to profile their existing customer base, building a picture of their preferences. That information is then used to target other potential customers who fit a similar profile.

Although this method is beyond the reaches of many smaller companies, your own existing customers can be used in the same way to detect trends towards certain media. Either simple face to face questions or a questionnaire, completed by 'phone or by mail, can give you the information you need to make a more considered decision.

Whatever you sell, whoever you sell to, you will find that your customers will be similar in certain ways. Discover these similarities and you will be in a position to choose your media with more certainty.

If, at the end of the day, there isn't too much to choose between a couple of titles, the measurement of **cost per thousand readers** covered is as good as any to help point you in the right direction. This simple measurement is calculated by taking the cost of a certain size of advertisement and dividing it by the circulation figure. Therefore, if paper A has a circulation of 10,000 and costs £100 for a particular advertisement, then the cost per thousand is £10, while paper B's 22,000 circulation and cost of £250 gives a cost per thousand of £11.36, making paper A the most effective choice.

All the same principles apply if you are choosing trade media rather than local newspapers. It may well be easier for you to establish a fairly clear readership trend. However, the most important point to focus on is which particular titles are actually read rather than simply received. Trade magazines, especially those which are delivered free of charge, have a habit of being left unread due to pressure of work, leaving the largest circulation figures of no benefit. Your customers will tell you whether they really find the magazine useful and readable.

## CHECKLIST 1 - FINDING THE CORRECT MEDIA

Ask these questions to help find the most suitable media to use.

**1**. What media are my competition using?

**2**. What is my target area and target customer?

**3**. Which title are the national companies using frequently?

**4**. Which title gives the most cost effective cost per thousand?

**5**. Which media do my existing customers read?

*C H A P T E R   3*

# Producing an advertisement that works

Let's assume then that you have found the media you feel most comfortable with for your

*Quick Tip*

If you have an advertisement prepared by an "in house" design studio, ask them to provide you with a bromide of the advert when completed. You will be able to use this in other media too and you can then be sure that reproduction will be good. Other titles using your advertisement copied from the first paper will be unable to reproduce your ad as well as the initial insertion, so it is well worth being prepared if you can be.

product or service. Where do you go from there? If you are thinking of advertising your product or service for the very first time, then you may not have produced an advertisement before.

Whether you are using local, regional or trade media you may well be able to use the *"in house"* studio facilities to produce your first advert. As a first step this is an acceptable low cost method of producing artwork. If you are lucky, the staff on the newspaper or magazine will be very experienced in putting together advertisements. However, as I mentioned a little earlier, they will lack particular experience of your product or maybe even your industry and marketplace. Because of this the resulting advertisement will only be as effective as the information you can supply to whoever is dealing with your project.

**As the saying goes, you get what you pay for.** It's wise to realise that you are unlikely to be produced an award winning advertisement for free. You should also be aware that advertisements produced for you by a newspaper or magazine may tend to be styled much like other advertisements produced *"in house"*. This is to be expected and is the trade off for getting artwork produced cheaply rather than spending more through an advertising agency or independent graphic designer.

You may have already had a number of good ideas regarding content or style of an advertisement for your product or service. There will have been advertisements that have caught your eye, made you laugh, or made you take a second look in the past. Hopefully these are the types of advertisement now finding their way into your *"Snatch File"*. Generally, the reason these advertisements have been so effective is likely to have been a powerful headline which attracted you in the first place.

**Browse through the papers and take a really good look at the advertising**. Don't just skip through the pages, but concentrate on each and every advertisement. Take a few minutes to think about what each advertisement is trying to achieve. *Put another way, what is the advertisement hoping to get you to do?*

Flick through any paper or magazine you'll see advertisements working well to generate enquiries and advertisements not producing the responses that their companies had anticipated. What's more, the effective ad could even be running side by side with the flop and they could even be trying to sell the same product. Hunt for the advertisements that jump out of the page and hit you between the eyes. The ads that make you pick up the 'phone or clip the coupon are the winners. When you come across the ads that don't make you take action, then you have most probably found a waste of money.

We will cover this point again, but quite simply an advertisement should always be attempting to convince the reader to take some sort of action. The action could be a number of things including:

- **To phone** for more information

- **To send** a coupon for more information

- **To try** a free sample

- **To visit** a shop soon

- **To buy** a product directly off the page

- **To use** a "money off" offer to purchase a product

Advertisements that lack any form of what is called a *"call to action"* will not be so effective in persuading the customer to make the next move. They will lack the killer punch and, as a result, will produce poorer responses. In such a competitive world you have to work pretty hard to get action. Miss the opportunity to push your potential customer at every stage and you'll miss the opportunity to create a new sales lead.

Whether you are designing your advertisement alone or being helped, the initial step in forming your campaign should be to establish your *"Unique Selling Point"*. The unique selling point of your product or service is something that you can offer that your competitors probably can't. For example, if you own a butchers shop and you have a home delivery service and your competitors don't - then this may be the point to highlight in your advertising to help differentiate your company from the opposition.

## AVOIDING THE TRAP ...

Many small businesses fall into a trap when they first advertise. In your local paper you may well find an advertisement that carries a company name at the top acting as the headline. The question to ask yourself when you see such an advertisement is *"what exactly is this company selling me?"* If you can't work it out within a few seconds as your eye passes over the page, then the chances are that it's not going to produce the most effective results.

An exception to this rule is when you are using advertising to strengthen the *"Corporate Image"*. To employ this type of advertising you generally need to be in a position to be able to allocate a budget towards advertising that may not necessarily produce results immediately, but which will help to build awareness for the future. When designing advertising in this style the company name or slogan is sometimes the most important element of the advert and can be allocated a great deal of prime space. You tend to see examples of this style of advertising from sponsors of events, in yearbooks and suchlike.

The important point to take on board here is that sometimes other, very much smaller businesses, treat their advertising in the *"corporate"* style and forget to highlight specific services or products. *"Corporate"* style advertising has its place, but not when you want to produce cost effective campaigns geared to selling particular items and when you need rapid results.

Of course, the argument regarding company names used as a headline is a little different if the name includes the products that you sell, such as *"Jones & Son Fencing Ltd"* for example. However, even though the headline may include an indication of your product, it is unlikely to include an offer of any kind - decreasing the impact you could have on the readers. Some companies are lucky enough to enjoy a strong level of awareness, either through constant advertising or maybe a high profile location. If this is the case and their advertising leads with their name, then they are in danger of being *"passed over"* by readers who, through familiarity, assume that they know the message in the ad already.

If *"Jones & Son"* had a special offer running for a free fence panel, maybe they would achieve more success if their headline reads something like:

### UNBEATABLE FREE FENCE PANEL OFFER!

The offer of the free fence panel would be their unique selling point. Unique selling points, or USPs as you may hear them referred to, can and do change, which is one reason why you should continually review your advertising.

**Headlines are very important.** It is said that an advertisement headline is read up to five times more than the actual words within the advert. Headlines needn't be at the top of the

advert of course. Looking through papers and magazines you will see many examples of headlines in different positions, either below a photograph, running alongside the ad or in other positions. A headline can also be different in other ways too, such as the use of white lettering out of a black background. This treatment is known as **REVERSE COPY**. Reverse copy can be effective but take a look at the publication where you are thinking of using your advert before you make your decision as *"Reverse"* has become more popular over the past few years and sometimes, if everyone is using that style, all the advertising tends to look similar.

The majority of readers - your target audience - don't spend hours pawing their way through a paper or magazine devouring the information on each and every page. You don't have long to impress a reader so give yourself the best possible chance of attracting their attention by creating the strongest possible targeted headline that will demand that your potential customer reads on through to the end of your ad.

*There are very few rules as to the length of a headline.* It is very much a case of if you think it sounds right then try it. Just remember that you really want the readers to be able to tell from the headline exactly what you are offering them, even without them having to plough through the rest of the ad. Questions work well as headlines too. Examples would be:

**PAYING TOO MUCH FOR YOUR INSURANCE?**

**LOOKING FOR A NEW SHED?**

**FED UP WITH HIGH HEATING COSTS?**

**OVER 25 AND LOOKING FOR A BETTER MORTGAGE DEAL?**

**DOG OWNER?**

**MOVING HOUSE WITHIN THE NEXT 6 MONTHS?**

These headlines leave you in no doubt whatsoever about who they are aimed at. For example, anyone who isn't going to move house within the next six months or so isn't going to be interested in the advertisement. That's fine, as the ad will have been specifically targeted only for the house movers. If you are thinking of moving house, then the headline would be likely to interest you.

You don't have to use just one headline either. You will see ads that seem to use a number of headlines, all saying slightly different things. **The use of multiple headlines is becoming more popular, especially when working with direct mail.** The first headline will be in a smaller typeface, followed by the main headline and then an additional line to explain more about the offer. The additional headline is useful if you are using a shorter main headline. An example of a multiple headline might be:

1. **Attention anyone looking to change their car in the next six months**

2. **THE GREATEST SECONDHAND CAR DEAL EVER**

3. **An opportunity to buy nearly new cars at very low prices, with full guarantees.**

Everyone creates advertisements in different ways. You may find a headline easier to write after you have written the rest of the ad. The words in the advertisement are called the **COPY**. Copy can be long or short and can flow or can be produced as short points (known as bullet points). Whichever words you decide to include in your advertisement, always keep in mind exactly who you are trying to attract.

That is to say, if you are aiming your product at housewives, don't use the kind of technical language that you may use in a letter to one of your suppliers. *I always like to write in the style that I would normally talk to a customer face to face.* That way I am fairly confident that my target market will understand whatever it is that I am trying to explain to them. I have found that this rule has worked well in the past. If you are in any doubt about the style of the words you use, then don't be frightened to test them out on family, friends or relations. Getting it wrong the first time and being able to put it right is by far a better way of going about it than realising it is wrong after the advert has appeared when you will have paid for your mistake.

Even if you haven't written the advertisement yourself, it is a good idea to test it before you go ahead if you can. If you have staff, they could be a very good representation of your target market - so use them. If you are having an advertisement produced for you, then try to get a couple of different approaches produced to choose from - as long as it isn't going to cost an arm and a leg.

## PICTURE THIS ...

I am sure that you've heard the saying "A picture is worth a thousand words". In your advertisement a good illustration is certainly a major plus. I say illustration because sometimes a photograph isn't as effective as it could be due to poor reproduction. It is important to assess the standard of reproduction of black and white photographs in the media you are hoping to use. These days with the development of printing techniques it isn't so much a problem and it is rarely of concern in magazines printed on glossy paper. However, in some smaller papers printed on less sophisticated machines and on a lower quality paper reproduction can be poor and a badly produced photograph will not enhance your advertisement too much.

If you have doubts that a photograph will reproduce well enough consider using a line drawing of your product. Unlike a photograph a line drawing will reproduce well in most media and you'll be able to use it time and time again on other projects such as product brochures, pricelists and other printed material.

Another reason for using a line drawing rather than a photograph would be when you find it difficult to get the right type of shot of your product. For example, you may need a winter scene in the summer or a summer scene in the winter, or you may need to show a particular type of customer who may be difficult to find in real life. Using a drawing in these circumstances will offer you far more flexibility. A drawing is also handy when you don't yet have the product to photograph but you would like to have an advertisement prepared ready for a specific date. This is particularly true if you are manufacturing an item and you have a prototype but no production model.

**If you do use an illustration or photograph in your ad, then make sure that it faces into and not out of the advert.** Photographs or illustrations which face out of the advertisement tend to encourage the reader's eye to wander out of the body of the ad, whilst photos facing into the ad pull the reader into the space a little more.

## MAKING THE ADVERTISEMENT WORK FOR YOU ...

Along with your words *(copy)* and illustration, the next step is to make certain that once you have managed to secure the interest of your potential customer, you leave them in no doubt what action they should take next. If you want them to call you to order your product or at least to talk to your sales team, then shout the message loud and clear. **Give your telephone number plenty of space.** Tell them to call now, today. Make it absolutely clear in your advertisement that you want to hear from them right now! As mentioned a little earlier, this is known as a *"call to action"* and if you aren't using words to strengthen the action your response may be less. Even a simple little thing such as an illustration of a telephone by your number will strengthen the call to action.

*Quick Tip*

When you have an illustration produced for you, try to have bromides of the work made if you can. Never send the original to a newspaper or magazine, because if it gets lost, you'll have to spend more to reproduce it again.

There are different options available to you to increase the number of telephone calls you receive from your ads. The most obvious is freephone which undoubtedly increases the number of responses you will generate. Like freepost, which we will mention later, freephone numbers may reduce the overall quality of the enquiries since it costs nothing for the customer to call. It therefore lowers the commitment that they have to make to you. However, you may feel that this is a worthwhile and acceptable added cost to attract those callers you really want to respond. A local call rate number also increases the number of enquiries but is of more use if you are promoting nationwide.

**Let's talk about another call to action - coupons.**

A coupon is an excellent method of generating controlled response into your business. However, if you are thinking of local press advertising it may not be for you as coupons aren't generally so effective when used closer to home. This is probably because potential customers tend to want to take action reasonably quickly when they are looking for items in a local press. *Cutting out a coupon and sending it three miles doesn't seem to make much sense.* That's another reason why your telephone number should be very prominent in a local ad.

A coupon may well be worth thinking about in other media though, if you are advertising nationally or in trade press for example. In fact, if you are aiming to generate response and are running ads without a coupon you really need to have a very good reason why. If your advert is too small for a coupon you will have an excuse, otherwise you may be struggling to justify the exclusion.

Once again, just like the telephone *"call to action"* you should try to strengthen up the coupon, encouraging more readers to take immediate action. Phrases such as *"send today"* or *"post now"* flashed on the coupon will increase its effectiveness.

The information you are looking to secure from the coupon will vary. In its very simplest form you will want a name and address, but there are a number of other decisions to make too.

For example, you may wish to contact your potential customer by telephone in which case you will want to try to encourage them to give you their telephone number. If you plan to follow up the contact by 'phone and you don't attempt to get a number you will be wasting a good deal of time and costing yourself extra money to retrieve each and every number.

*You'll never get every telephone number but at least you'll get a percentage.* Some people won't give numbers because they don't want to be telephoned, but some will not give their number because, invariably, the space for the telephone number is the last thing on the coupon and is simply ignored. People are lazy, so after they have filled in their address details, the rest sometimes isn't even considered.

One easy way around this, and a simple method that will increase the percentage of numbers you receive is to **request the telephone number after the name and before the address.** This way the information is more a part of the coupon and tends to be filled in more naturally as people are working their way through.

Incidentally, don't forget to request the postcode separately too as it can save you money if you are able to use bulk mailings in the future. It will also enable you to get the information to your customer more quickly and, if you decide to hold the information on a database, will give you an easy method of pinpointing and retrieving your customer information in the future.

## INCREASING THE NUMBER OF REPLIES ...

As we have already mentioned, a freephone telephone number will increase the number of leads you receive. The next important decision is whether you wish to use a freepost address for your customers to use. **A freepost address will also increase the number of enquiries you receive but, as with a freephone number, you may find that the quality level of the leads is less than if you had asked the customer to pay for a stamp**. As with a freephone facility, a freepost address lessens the customer commitment. Details about freepost and other business reply services are available from your local post office who can direct you to a special department set up to help businesses like your own get the most out of the services on offer.

**Make your coupon as big as you can within the limits of your budget.** A tiny coupon that customers find difficult to complete will reduce the response rate. If you are having real difficulties trying to fit a coupon into a small advertisement and you would prefer to receive enquiries through the post rather than by telephone ask the customer to write a short note or maybe look at the possibility of making the whole of the advertisement the coupon so that it is easier to fill in. But beware, even asking your customers to write a short note is placing a further obstacle in the way of replies and you will see a lower response rate. On the other hand, the replies you do receive should be that much better quality.

You will want to estimate the level of enquiries that you are aiming for. If you would rather receive hundreds of replies and then try to convert them include all the elements that will encourage more leads. However, if you would rather just generate a few replies that you are more confident of converting into sales, then build in some elements that will mean the customer has to show a degree of commitment to receive your details. If you were trying to sell a product *"off the page"*, you would, of course, include all the elements you could to try to increase the response rates.

Bear in mind your capacity to follow up the number of leads you generate. There is simply no point in creating far more leads than you can comfortably deal with properly. By the time you have found time to follow them up, the customers may have changed their minds or bought elsewhere. One difficulty in producing large quantities of enquiries is trying to spot the ones which will produce the results.

In the same way that a picture of a telephone will help to strengthen a call to action, **a pair of scissors** and a strong dotted line really does make sure that the customer is in no doubt about what he or she should do next with the coupon.

## ADDING THE FINISHING TOUCHES ...

A dotted line on your coupon is a form of border and borders are very important for an advertisement. Try experimenting with different types of border to get your advertisement noticed in the paper or magazine. It's surprising the effect a strong border can have. *It can really help to make the advert stand out.*

A border doesn't necessarily have to be a black line. Making your advertisement slightly smaller than the space you have bought will have the effect of producing a white border around your ad, which will stand out more on the page due to its less cluttered surroundings.

> **Quick Tip**
>
> You don't have to cram as much information as you possibly can into your advertisement. By using what is known as "white space" to give your advert room to breathe, you may well find that the points you are trying to get across will have more impact.

Flashes are another tool to use when you want to get a special point across. Starbursts with *"Free", "Guaranteed"* etc. can help to get your ad read in the first place and increase response.

There are very few rules in marketing and this is particularly true of advertising. You don't quite know what is going to work and what isn't until you try it, so, if you come up with a very different idea and you can afford to experiment - *have a go*. However, if you are looking for your first campaign to produce you concrete results I would suggest you try to stick to the principles that have worked over the years. If you do decide to try something out of the ordinary, using an odd position may give you the edge. For example, you could run the advertisement upside down, at an angle or on its side for more effect. Using this approach usually means that you will have to get permission from the publishers though, as sometimes they aren't too keen on the more outrageous or creative approaches as they make it harder to sell advertising space on the rest of the page.

Clearly it helps if you have a solid message to support your creative idea. One of the most obvious uses for an upside down advertisement would be for a travel agent selling Australian holidays - I'm sure you get the message!

To recap then, producing an effective advertisement depends on a number of key factors, the most important of which must always be the understanding of what you are selling and to whom. Apart from this there are other, more specific details to ensure you get right. They are:

- **The Headline - make it attention getting and powerful**

- **The Copy - gain interest and make the customer want to buy the product.**

- **The Action - once you've gained the interest, make sure you lead the customer onto the next step.**

### CHECKLIST 2 - PUTTING THE ADVERTISEMENT TOGETHER

**1**. Have I got a strong headline which will attract my target customer?

**2**. Are my words (copy) strong enough to interest the reader? Have I included my USP (unique selling point)?

**3**. If I have used an illustration or photograph, will they reproduce well and are they in the right position. Are they facing into the ad?

**4**. Does my advertisement let the reader know what to do next? Have I used a "call to action"?

**5**. Is my coupon or telephone number strong enough?

**6**. Have I used flashes to highlight any important points?

**7**. Does my advertisement have a strong border?

*CHAPTER 4*

# Using your advertisement in the most cost-effective way

Once you've made your decision about where to advertise and you have an idea about the type of advertisement that you would like to use there are a number of other points to consider. They are:

**A. How large is the budget that I am willing to allocate to my campaign?**

**B. How long do I want my campaign to run?**

**C. How large do my advertisements need to be to get my message across properly?**

**D. Where do I want my advertisements to appear?**

*The key question is how much to spend.* Usually, of course, the answer is as little as possible to get the maximum amount of coverage. If you are convinced that advertising is for you, then it might be wise to budget for a larger figure than you first thought of. The reason being you have to give the promotion a chance to work.

It may seem pretty obvious, but generally advertising is more effective the more you do of it - until you reach a level where the returns start to diminish. Plan to run your campaign over some weeks if you can, to gain the confidence of the readers as you become more familiar to them. Sometimes readers need to see the advertisement a number of times before they really take notice.

You will hear all of this from the paper's sales representative and, generally speaking, they will be offering good advice. Don't be tempted to run a huge advert for just one week, as you may well be disappointed, especially if you haven't had the opportunity to test the content of the advert before it appears. If you do decide to use smaller sizes, the position of the ad becomes even more important - something that we will be discussing later.

Ideally you should aim to have your advertisement seen at least five or six times in the same paper, either every week, or if you want to stretch the campaign longer, maybe just once every other week. However, running the ad even just every other week will dilute the awareness that you are hoping to build.

You may be able to afford larger sizes of advertisement. However, the ad doesn't necessarily need to be the same size throughout the whole campaign. I'm sure that you will have seen advertising on TV that begins as a 60 second commercial which runs for six weeks and then is cut shorter to 30 seconds and then reduced even further to a 15 second ad. You can plan your advertising in a similar way.

For example, you could begin with a quarter page advert for four weeks and then reduce the size to an eighth page. As long as the ad either stays the same or has the same strong message this method of stretching the budget can be effective.

You may have the product range or the type of service which suit a series of advertisements built around a theme and which can run for a number of weeks, increasing both product and company awareness at the same time. If you are promoting a number of different products or a variety of services, but would like to use a standard format throughout the campaign, try to produce a design that specific items can be worked into. That way the readers are given more opportunities to absorb a general message and, at the same time, individual product points can be highlighted to generate specific interest.

A good example of this style of promotion might be a business such as a Garden Centre, where the item featured may vary according to the season, but where the centre itself wished to build awareness and increase its profile, becoming more easily recognised in the local press. The general design of the advertisement could remain the same throughout the campaign, while the specific product and its features changed as and when necessary. *Very strong, unique borders would be just one way of making sure that the advertisement had a theme.*

**There is also another way to make your advertising more effective on the page**. You can choose a size or a shape that will give you optimum exposure. For example, you can sometimes save money by designing your advertisement just a little smaller than a full page. If your advertisement is a column less wide and a column less high than a full page you will generally find your ad is the only one on the page with surrounding editorial, as finding a very small ad to fill the gap may be difficult.

In fact, even if another ad did appear on the page, it would be so small in comparison to your own that it wouldn't have a detrimental effect. Using this method, especially if you have a powerful advertisement, will provide you with the impact of a full page without paying full page costs. In addition, with some interesting editorial around your ad, you may even have a higher awareness level than if you had taken the full page yourself. There will be a certain size in the paper which will dominate the page. Decide what that size is and you might not have to pay full page prices to create the impact you need.

*Quick Tip*

If you are buying space at a premium rate for the special positions such as the TV page, then it is even more important to be sure that the extra you are paying is worth it. You won't know that unless you have some idea of what response you might expect from an advert placed in a standard position.

*ODD SHAPED ADS MAY CAUSE MORE INTEREST*

Odd shapes can sometimes work to make your advertising more effective too, especially if you intend to take longer runs in the paper. For example, a thin advertisement right across the page can be effective. *Be warned however, don't try to be too clever* or you run the danger of the only person who thinks it's great being yourself. If you think that an odd or less conventional shape may work, then simply mock up an ad quickly and place it in an existing paper to get a feel of just how it will look. This is the closest you'll be able to get to a trial run before it starts costing you real money.

*Be careful with the use of humour too* - what may seem funny to you might not seem funny to the readers, especially if the humour is linked to a product that they don't understand too well. Being too creative can sometimes have its drawbacks, as the product benefits get lost in a beautiful or intricate style, so try to keep it as simple as you can - to start with at any rate. You can create the award winning advert later on, when there's plenty of money in the bank, but for now try to go with a reasonably safe approach, especially if you need to get results quickly.

**Quick Tip**

If you intending to use large ad spaces, don't commit yourself to too many insertions too quickly. Large spaces can be expensive and so you'll want to be sure that your ad works before blasting away!

Finally, try to come up with a few different advertisements if it is the first time you have produced them. Then, as I mentioned previously, test them on your staff, family and friends. Try not to lose your aim of producing the most effective ad possible and guard against a *"Not Invented Here"* syndrome. Listen to the criticisms you receive since they are from the type of people who may be customers. If necessary take the good bits from a couple of adverts and try to work them in together to produce the most effective version. Remember too that generally advertisements have a short lifespan and that you will almost certainly develop better and more effective ads in the future, so don't try to create the perfect ad the first time out. Just make sure that you are reasonably confident that you will be able to attract your target customer.

Soon I'll be running through the steps you can take to monitor how well your advertisement is performing and so decide whether to change the ad, increase the run or stop altogether. But for now, here's a few methods to use to make your advertising even more cost effective.

## GETTING THE MOST FOR YOUR MONEY ...

Whenever you decide to book advertising of any kind, you should always be conscious of getting the most for your money. Every pound you save in discounts can be ploughed back into your campaign, so you should start with the aim of getting the best possible deals the very first time you buy.

*There are two basic methods used to book advertising.* The first method is to book a campaign over a period of weeks or months. The paper or magazine obviously prefer this method as they are securing a reasonable order for little effort. There are advantages of booking in this way for you also. Firstly, you spend less time on the task since it can be wrapped up with one meeting or one or two phone calls. Secondly, you know exactly when and where your advertisements are going to appear so you are in a better position to be able to control any enquiries more effectively. Thirdly, you may only have to pay one account and finally, you should automatically enjoy the increased awareness that an extended run in one title can provide.

However, most small businesses cannot afford or are unwilling to commit expenditure over a longer period of time, preferring to take each week as it comes and monitor their spending against results. If you are in this position you may wish to look at alternative methods of booking space.

Wherever and whenever you first buy advertising space, be sure to ask for a *"first time advertisers"* discount. Generally, there will be discounts to be had, so try to obtain them. The only time that you may have difficulty in negotiating a discount is if you are using a very strong newspaper or magazine having very little serious competition in the area. In this case you may find you are unlucky as they may have a policy of not discounting - they probably won't need to.

If you are having difficulty securing a discount, then you could try to obtain the *"agency discount"* yourself. The agency discount is the amount given automatically to advertising agencies when they book space for their clients. It's how they make their money on the deal. If you are not using an agency, you could suggest that the discount is given directly to you. The agency discount is a percentage often given away and one easy enough to *"lose"* off the cost without too much trouble. It's a cheeky way of obtaining a few pounds off the cost, so approach the subject in a light-hearted way - it may work. If you are lucky (or clever ) enough to obtain this discount you will find that they will range from 10% to 15% and so are very worthwhile.

The second method of booking advertising space is the *"Late Space"* method. In the same way that you may have sat next to holidaymakers on a plane who have paid 30% less for the same break because they booked the day before, you can get significant discounts if you book your advertising on or close to the publication deadline.

Although this method tends to be more cost effective it can result in your campaign being less structured as you have to react to space availability as and when it happens. It could mean, for example, that you have a run of three adverts and then aren't offered cheaper space until three weeks later. Having said this, you can, if you wish, top up your late space bookings with standard rate space, but only if you are really on top of your promotions.

When using the late space method of booking it is even more important to build a strong relationship with your newspaper contact as you are going to be more reliant on him or her to offer you the best deals. Your initial message to whoever is handling your account should be that although you are interested in trying advertising, which you believe will be successful for your product or service, you don't have a huge budget and you need to be careful. At the same time, however, emphasise the fact you will be more than willing to commit additional funds if you can satisfy yourself that this method of promotion will work for you.

The next step if you are aiming to use late space, is to suggest to the salesperson that you should send in your advertisement which you hope they might be able to use if they have any late space available.

*"Late Space"* is simply that. A hole that has to be filled in the paper and filled quickly. It can become available for a number of reasons such as:

- Due to an editorial decision the paper has been increased in size by another 4 pages and they are trying to sell off the last few pages before deadline.

- An advertiser who is required to pre-pay has failed to do so and his ad has been pulled, or

- An advertisement has been lost or has not arrived at the paper in time for printing deadlines.

*Action Point*

If you are considering an advertising campaign for the first time, try to produce a budget to work to. If you have a budget in mind, you will be less likely to overspend.

Another reason is simply that the newspaper is struggling to fill its advertising quota. This is quite often the case, especially in difficult trading times. If this is so, you already have a very strong position.

**The most important point about taking advantage of late space is that it will work most effectively for you if you can have a ready to use advertisement at the paper before it is required.**

Because you will need to be able to produce an advertisement for a newspaper to use at short notice, then you will most probably have to present the paper with the complete advertisement, or *"finished artwork"* as it is known. There are always specialist typesetters that will produce an advertisement for you, and these days with the development of computerised systems, you'll be amazed at the sophisticated results you can achieve by using such a business.

Generally, the typesetters will be used to putting advertisements together and so you can take advantage of their creative input which is certain to come far more cheaply than if you used an Advertising Agency. Make sure that your advertisement is produced to a size that could be used in the paper of your choice by getting hold of the technical details from the paper and making whoever is producing your ad aware of the size it should be.

After your ad has been prepared and you are happy with it, then it is time to talk to the newspapers in which you are interested in taking space.

This method of booking advertising space is designed to get you the best deals and so you have to be *"up front"* with the newspaper representatives and tell them that you can only advertise with them if they can manage to come up with the right cost savings for you. Let the representative know that you have an advertisement *"just sitting here waiting to be used"* and that you wondered whether it would be a good idea to send it to them *"just in case they may be able to use it in the future"*.

The idea that there is a ready to use advertisement waiting to fill a gap, or get them out of a hole is usually of great interest to the representative - and so it should be. If he or she can get you to try advertising once and they can prove to you that it has worked, you are most probably going to repeat it and, over a period of time, you are going to be worth quite a bit to both them and to the paper. As they say, from little acorns.... In the end, both of you are going to be happy.

## MAKING THE FIRST MOVE ...

Either send the advertisement to the paper or arrange for the representative to call and pick it up if they are local. If he or she does call in to pick it up, make sure that you are around so that you can begin to start building a relationship with them. As I have mentioned before, just like all relationships in business, the relationship with the advertising representative is very important. Build a good, strong relationship and he or she can save you a good deal of money over a period of time. They can also make sure you receive the best positions too, something we will be covering soon. *In short, they could be very important to you.*

It is important for the representative to know as much as they can about exactly what you are looking to achieve from your advertising, so, if they don't ask, tell them. You will want them to be able to spot features and other promotions being run in the paper which may be of interest to you but which they themselves may not be handling.

If you send the advertisement to the paper, give your contact a call after a couple of days just to make sure that they have received it. This also gives you another opportunity to start to build a relationship if you have not met face to face.

**After you are sure that they have received the advertisement - wait.** Normally it won't be too long before you get a call to make you an offer. If you do wait for a little while and hear nothing, and you are keen to start advertising, then make enquiries to check that the advertisement is still around ready to be used and that your contact is still with the paper.

Advertising representatives do tend to come and go somewhat. You may have to deal with a number of them until you find one that will stick around for a while. The representatives who have been at the paper for some time are generally the ones to try to build a relationship with, because the chances are that they are good at what they do, are happy in their jobs and will be around for some time to come.

The call that eventually comes will inform you that there is a space to be filled in the paper at short notice and that they can fill this space at a discount. *Bingo, you are starting to save money on your advertising straight away.*

Before we go any further, let me mention that it is important for you to have received, and have to hand, the cost details from the newspapers you are thinking of using. Their pricelist is called the **RATE CARD**. You'll need the rate card to make sure that you really are getting a good deal and that the representative isn't pulling the wool over your eyes.

*Quick Tip*

If you can, give yourself a little thinking time when you are buying late space by asking the salesperson to call back in 10 minutes for a decision. It's too easy to say yes on the spur of the moment and regret it afterwards.

**What do you do when you get the call for your first cheap advertising space?** Well, listen carefully to what's being offered and don't necessarily take the first deal that comes along. It's important to understand that the first deal you strike with your contact will set the standard for all the deals in the future. You will normally be told the space available along with the cost and, just as importantly, what the rate card cost should be. If your contact does not volunteer this information, get it as you may want to keep it on file for the future. Apart from anything else, it's a nice feeling when you can sit down and calculate exactly what you have saved off the cost of an advertising campaign. *If you are working for someone else, it's a good way of showing them your value!*

You should bear in mind that if you are keen to follow the cheap space route, then you need to be securing substantial discounts to compensate for the fact that you might not be enjoying the constant awareness that a more structured advertising plan can produce.

If you are only getting offered a minimal discount, you may as well adopt the more structured campaign approach as you will generally be entitled to a discount for a series of advertisements in any case. So, make sure that the discounts you are achieving are worth it. In the past when I have adopted this method of buying space, I have been receiving discounts of anything from **45% to 80% off** the rate card cost, so don't sell yourself short and stick out for a better deal if you can afford the time to wait.

Another thing to bear in mind when booking late space is that the space offered may not be exactly the same as the size to which you had produced your artwork. This doesn't matter too much unless you are determined to only use the size of ad you have prepared. The paper will be able to adapt or possibly reset your ad for you, or they will be able to increase or decrease the size of your artwork to fit whatever is available.

What is very important however, is to make sure that, if possible, you get to see a proof of the new version before it is printed, since mistakes can happen during the resetting process and they may redesign your advertisement in a way that you feel makes the ad far less effective. Try to get to see the new ad if you can, but bear in mind that we are talking about late space and so there may not be the time to get a copy to you. Sometimes you will just have to trust their judgement and let it go. That is one of the negatives connected to the late space option.

We'll be talking a little more about saving money soon, but for now let's consider the power of securing a good position for your advert.

## BEING IN THE RIGHT PLACE AT THE RIGHT TIME ...

Positions are very important and some of the more effective ones may carry a surcharge. For example, a front page or back page spot or a position on a page on your own *(solus)* would generally cost more because they are prime spaces. You can, however, make your advertising more effective straight away for no extra cost just by asking for your ad to appear on a right hand page.

You'll realise when you look through a paper that you generally look at the right hand side page first - **so, if you can get on a right hand page, all the better**. Even more effective is to be on an early page in the paper and the best of both worlds is to be on an early right hand page. **Pages 3, 5 and 7** should be your target. If you can get onto an early right hand page you will be increasing your effectiveness, but you'll increase it even further if you can obtain a top right hand position. **The right hand page** is the one which catches the eye, but the top right hand side of the page is the first to be scanned in many cases, so try to be there if you can.

One exception to this rule is when you are running a coupon on your advert. Then you would be better off in the **bottom right hand position** as there are fewer cuts to make to remove the coupon. If you are running an advertisement with a coupon you should also specify an outside edge of a page. *Having an advert with a coupon tucked away in the centre of the page will reduce the response considerably.* This is simply because it is far less easy to cut out a coupon in that position and also that it could mean removing an area which includes news editorial overleaf. This is something readers are sometimes unwilling to do, especially if the newspaper or magazine is shared with other people in the family or at the workplace. Basically, the less a reader has to make a mess of the page, the better.

Right hand pages, whether early or not, shouldn't be subject to a surcharge. However, you may find them harder to obtain as they'll get booked up fairly quickly by the advertisers running a campaign. Also, the representatives will tend to try to position their regular customers on the most effective pages - and quite rightly so. This is another strong reason for you to get friendly with your contact at the paper.

You will hear the term *"Run of Paper"* or ROP as it is more commonly known. This simply means being positioned within the paper alongside editorial, or anywhere other than the classified section. If you don't specify a position, then your advertisement will be placed into a run of paper position.

**By not at least asking for a better position you are playing Russian roulette with your advertising.** You could find yourself absolutely anywhere in the newspaper if you don't specify where you would prefer to be. If you are selling computer equipment, for example, you won't necessary want to be positioned on the page which carries a column which is mainly read by the older generation. Leave it to chance and you could well be.

Occasionally when you are offered late space you will find that the availability is on a particular feature which hasn't yet been filled or sometimes even within the classified section. That's all right as long as you are fully aware of the facts and you feel that your advertisement will still be effective in such a position. Unless you specifically ask, then you may not be told where the space actually is. If you don't keep on top of this you might find that you have spent money on an advertisement which is on a page which really won't work for you. So, if you don't think that your advertisement for Lawnmowers will work so well on a Backpain feature, don't run with it!!

Another position that you may wish to consider is the *"Earpiece"*. Earpieces are the small advertisement spaces at the top of the front page, near the banner title of the paper. They are very visible and generally quite effective if you can afford to run with them for a while. Unfortunately, you may well find that the earpieces are not available on late space as they are quite popular and may be booked up for weeks on end. However, if you are lucky enough to secure one you will find them useful for increasing general awareness. You may also wish to consider them to kick off a promotion or even to highlight your larger advertisement inside the paper. For example, you could run the earpiece to announce a special offer, such as:

**FENCE PANELS ONLY £9.99 EACH**

**SEE OUR ADVERTISEMENT ON PAGE 13.**

Earpieces are quite small and so you will have to ensure that you pack a powerful message in what will be a very limited space. **Short, sharp copy is the key here.**

The television page can be a strong page in a newspaper too and, because of this, it is another that sometimes carries a surcharge. If you cannot get onto an early right, then the TV page may be the next best bet. However, it is wise to get to know the paper and find out for yourself whether the TV page is actually read. These days there are so many papers and magazines carrying the TV listings that it would be impossible for them all to be used frequently, so, if you are looking to use a local paper, ask around to discover whether they use the TV guide, just to give yourself a little peace of mind.

## THE BEST OF BOTH WORLDS ...

*Can you secure a good position even if you are getting a deal on late space?* The answer is yes you can, sometimes. However, I have found that the longer you have been doing business with the paper or magazine, the more chance of getting the position that you request. It's basically all down to relationships again. But, based on the principle that you never get anything unless you ask for it, you should always ask for a good position whenever you book any ad. **You'll be amazed how many people never dream of asking for a special position, so you may be lucky every time!**

Getting the very best deals for your advertising does take time, but you will go some way towards making your promotions more cost-effective and stretching your budgets if you can remember these important points and try to action them at each stage of your planning:

- **Produce an advertisement ready to use.**

- **Make contact with your representative and build a relationship in the paper before you need them.**

- **Know what you should be paying and what would be a good deal for you.**

- **After you have booked your space, at a rate you are happy with, then try and get the best position you can.**

## THE NEGOTIATION ...

To help you further, here's an example of what might happen when you receive the first call offering you advertising space. Mr Jones has sent an advertisement into the newspaper and is now about to receive a call from his representative:

**REP**        Good morning Mr Jones, I've got the ad you sent to me in front of me and I've got some late space that has just come up. Are you still interested in using it?

**MR JONES**   Yes, thanks for calling. As I said to you before I'm keen to try advertising and I'm keen to try your paper in particular, it's just the costs that I cannot afford at the moment. As you know I'm a small business and I have to be careful about what I spend right now. What sort of deal have you got for me?

**REP**        Well, the ad you sent to me is a quarter page size which normally costs £350. However, I have some space to fill and I can do it for £300.

**MR JONES**   Well, it's going in the right direction, but quite honestly I don't think that I could afford that right now. It's a pity really, because I think it will work for me but I really need to be sure before I commit more money. How about I give you £150 for the space?

**REP**        I just couldn't come down that low. Would £260 make the difference?

**MR JONES**   Look, I really want to give this a go. I suppose I could go to £195 but no more.

**REP**        OK, let's put it in for that and see how we get on.

*Quick Tip*

Always remember, first priority is the price you are paying, then the position of the advert and then securing editorial along with the ad.

**MR JONES**  I'm happy with that, as long as you can get me a good position on a right hand page. We both want to give the advertisement the best possible chance of succeeding don't we? How about page 3?

In this example, Mr Jones hasn't advertised before, so the chances are that he isn't going to be offered a truly magnificent offer first time around. However, with just a little negotiation he has reduced the price of the advertisement considerably - *not just important for this one ad but also for the future.* Furthermore, Mr Jones has asked for a position that will make his ad more effective and which will also set the standard for the placement of future advertisements too.

## STRETCHING THE POINT FURTHER ...

After you have managed to get a good discount and a preferred position, can you make your advertisement even more cost effective?

**Once again the answer is yes, you can.**

When you have agreed a price for your advertisement and you have secured a position that will give the ad a good chance of success, you can then make further savings if you are willing to extend your advertising. You may get a reasonable deal for booking a series of advertisements but it is unlikely to be as attractive as a deal for a *"one off"* late space ad. The key now is to turn that *"one off"* ad into a series and achieve a further discount along the way. Returning to our telephone conversation the next stage may be:

**MR JONES**  Just as a matter of interest, if I took the same advertisement for, say three weeks, what price could you give me then?

**REP**  For three weeks, I could go to £175 I suppose.

**MR JONES**  And for six weeks?

**REP**  £150.

**MR JONES**  I tell you what, I really think that this could work for me, so I'll tell you what I'll do. Give me a rate of £135 a time and an early right hand position and I'll run it for six weeks. What do you say?

The advertisement should have cost £350 at rate card. From £350, Mr Jones negotiated a discount which eventually reduced the price to £195 and then got a further discount down to £135 when he suggested running a series of advertisements. He has saved himself a fair amount of money, not bad for a few minutes work, and for his first time of asking.

For the moment, let's spend a few minutes looking a little closer at the way the deal was achieved. Earlier in the book I mentioned that you should never buy advertising space until you are ready to do so. Mr Jones remembered that and what's more and just as importantly, he took control of the situation and didn't allow himself to be sold to. He turned the situation around so that he was suggesting the deal in the end, a deal that he was happy with.

*Notice also that Mr Jones didn't ask for a rate for six weeks straight away.* If he had he may well have been offered the same rate as the three week rate he was given. So, by asking for rates a little at a time he was eventually offered more discounts.

When you decide to take charge and to tell the paper how much you are willing to pay, do remember that although you can offer a price as low as you like, for your very first advertisement you shouldn't offer a ridiculously low amount as there will be a lower limit beyond which the salesperson will not be able to go - at least not for the first advert. Later on, when you are in a stronger position, you may well be able to get even bigger discounts.

*Quick Tip*
If you produce a set of bromides of your adverts, keep them together and make sure that you record exactly where you are sending them, so that you have a chance of them being returned. It can be an expensive affair to produce complete artwork and so you will want to use them more than once if possible.

*C H A P T E R   5*
# Managing a successful advertising campaign

The moment your first advertisement appears you become a target for every advertising representative in the area. As soon as the new papers are in circulation, every rep worth their salt will be scanning their competitors' papers looking for the first time advertiser. When they have spotted you, you'll be at the top of their hit list for sure.

If your business is located in an area that has just one or two papers serving it, then you'll probably be able to manage the calls quite easily. However, if you are in a large city with a number of competing newspapers, or you are advertising in trade papers and magazines, then you could receive a large number of calls all asking you the same question - **do you want to repeat your advertisement with us?**

You now have an opportunity, if you are ready to take it, for an extended advertising campaign. I say if because you may not know whether your first advertisement has worked for you before you start to hear from other papers. You are likely to receive calls the same day your advert appears. **The golden rule must be not to commit yourself until you are pretty sure that your promotion is proving worthwhile.** The temptation is to get carried away and start booking every space offered, especially if they seem like good deals - remember, in most cases the deals will still be there next week too, so slow down and take the time to make the right decision.

Going back to what we said about buying when the price is right for you, this is the time when you can make large savings if you have negotiated a good deal right at the very start. Obviously, different papers have different circulation figures and different target audiences so you may not be dealing with like for like, but you can certainly use the first deal to influence the amount you pay in other papers.

**In other words, once you have secured an acceptable deal to start your advertising, you will want to use it as a barometer for other deals offered to you in the future.**

If, when you are looking to place your first advertisements, the paper is unwilling to accept your space offer feeling that they could sell it for more, you may be able to take an *"option"* on it. That is to say you can reserve it and take it unless they can sell the space for a higher amount before the closing deadline. Make absolutely sure that you know when an *"option"* has become a firm booking, since if you don't, you could find yourself with higher bills than you had anticipated. Your contact at the paper should call you to confirm that it is running.

## BUT, BEFORE YOU PLOUGH AHEAD ...

When you are ready to start advertising, there are a couple of other important jobs which will ensure that the programme goes as smoothly as possible and that you are getting the most for your money.

Firstly, it is important, especially if you are considering the late space option, to put into place a **"bookings numbering system"** for your advertising. The reason is this: whenever you book advertising space you will eventually receive an invoice for that advertisement. If you are only booking a few adverts each month then that is relatively easy to manage, but as soon as you start placing advertisements in a number of different publications, or the same advertisement in different papers in the same group, the invoices become less easy to identify and to clear for payment.

If you are constantly doing deals to get the best price, then you will have an awful lot of information about prices, special positions etc. which will be almost impossible to keep your finger on unless it is written down somewhere. When an invoice is received which is higher than you expected (which can happen quite often), you will need to have handy the dates and times of conversations and prices agreed to ensure that you are paying only what you sanctioned.

To keep tabs on this situation, simply introduce a booking number for each advertisement you place and let the paper know that you expect to see that number on the invoice. A number will quickly highlight which advertisement is which and will save you a good deal of time. You may wish to create an advertisement booking form to help you keep track of how you are doing. Such a form would generally have the following information included:

| DATE | BOOKING NO. | SIZE OF ADVERT | PUBLICATION | CONTACT | ADVERT BOOKING COST | VOUCHER COPY | TOTAL COST |
|------|-------------|----------------|-------------|---------|---------------------|--------------|------------|
| 8/12 | 00121 | 8 x 7 TOP RIGHT | THE CHRONICLE | JOE - TEL 09421 | £40 | ✓ | £40 |
| | | | | | | | |
| | | | | | | | |

**A.** Date of booking

**B.** Booking Number

**C.** Size of Advert and any Special Positions agreed

**D.** Publication

**E.** Contact, Tel No and Fax No

**F.** Amount Paid

**G.** Voucher Copy received

**H.** Total Spent to date

This form includes all the information you would need to track your expenditure and to check that discounts negotiated are appearing correctly on the invoices you receive.

You can also use the form as a reminder of the prices paid when buying space again. This is always important to make sure that you don't lose any advantage you may have gained in the past by booking space which is slightly more expensive each time, moving you closer to the rate card prices each week.

**The voucher copy is also important as a control.** A voucher copy is the copy of the publication in which your advertisement appeared. You may be sent it along with the invoice. Sometimes you'll only receive the page on which your ad appeared, but more often than not you will get the whole publication. The voucher copy is the control you need to ensure that any special positions you secured are actually used. It also gives you the opportunity to check that your advertisement has been set properly if you haven't been given the opportunity to see a proof.

Don't keep all the publications you receive or you'll find yourself with a huge pile of paper in the corner or under the desk. Instead, cut out your advertisement or keep the page on which you appear and put together a scrapbook to use as a history file. Apart from keeping all your advertising in neat and tidy order it will also give you a running record of what you have done and when, especially if you remember to date them. It will also serve as an important document if you ever decide to use an outside agency or if you employ a marketing specialist in the future as they will immediately be able to see the history of your advertising. *Trying to explain to them the styles of your advertising three years ago without a copy of an ad will take an awful lot longer!*

Another important task when you embark on an advertising campaign is to let any staff you have know about it. This is, of course, especially important for any staff who are going to be either taking the telephone calls or dealing with letters or coupons generated from the advertising. Your staff need to see a copy of the advertisement so that they know about any special offers you may be running and so, if possible, they can have a copy of the advert in front of them when they are talking to customers.

There's nothing more embarrassing than blasting away with a major promotion without first informing your staff. Apart from sounding so unprofessional when a customer calls and hears *"offer, what offer?"*, your staff will feel frustrated and angry about being kept in the dark. Believe me … I know from past experience (or should I say inexperience!).

## HOW DO YOU KNOW WHETHER IT'S WORKING OR NOT? …

At the same time as keeping your staff informed, you should also create monitoring systems so that you will be able to make a decision about the effectiveness of the campaign.

**Why do you need to have a formal monitoring system in place?** Isn't it enough to be able to get a *"feel"* for what is happening? Well, it is true that you can run on *"gut feel"*, but at the end of the day, the only way to really know how effective a campaign has been is to have the figures readily available. **In the cold light of day the statistics can't lie.**

Later in the book I will be covering exhibitions and the fact that they can be as busy as you want them to be. In the same way, different people's views of results from advertising can be very different indeed. Your salesman may think that an ad has been very successful after pulling six enquiries whereas you were hoping for at least three times that amount. So, when you ask the question *"how's the new ad doing?"* and you get the answer *"fine"*, it's maybe less precise than you would want to be a basis for spending more.

Another very good reason for keeping a monitoring system for your enquiries is that it will allow you to spot trends, not just from ad to ad, but also over a longer period. Your system shouldn't just include replies from your advertising though. It should cover all enquiries from whatever source they are generated. **This is one reason why it is so important that the question *"where did you first hear of us?"* is always asked of new customers**.

If you do log all types of enquiries, sometimes you'll be able to identify new marketing opportunities too. For example, when a new type of enquiry, maybe generated through PR activity, keeps popping up in the system. If you see new enquiries coming from a new source time after time, then you should look at them closely and consider whether you can do more work in what may be excellent areas of new potential.

Implementing a monitoring system can be as easy as simply writing down all the replies to advertising that you receive, either over the telephone or through the post. To make sure that you are getting a more detailed picture however, your advertising needs to be coded to highlight the source.

**Coding your advertising is very simple**. If you are using a coupon response mechanism then place a code in the bottom right hand of the coupon, within the area to be cut out by the customer. Codes can be anything that you want them to be, but generally, the shorter the better. Code systems can be based on date of advertisements (01/05/95) or, if you are using different media, simply by adding the identification tag of the publication (NS0195).

But what if you don't use a coupon? How can you then identify enquiries easily? Again it is quite simple. If you are encouraging the customer to write in for information then add a department number to the address. For example:

**Widgets Ltd**
**Dept NS0195**
**etc, etc**

If you are hoping that the customer will telephone you, then you can again ask them for the code inserted somewhere within the advertisement.

*Action Point*

If your company employs others who should know about the promotional plans, make time to let them know what is happening and when. It doesn't have to be a meeting. It could be by way of a newsletter or simple note. People like to be kept informed. It's good for morale and essential for effective communication.

Another method to monitor enquiries is to direct all the telephone replies to a single named individual in the company. This can be less effective if the individual is otherwise engaged at the time the calls are received. *A simple answer to this problem is to use the name of an employee you haven't got!!* This way everyone knows that when the telephone rings and the customer asks to speak to Rupert, then it is an enquiry of a particular type. This method is quite effective, especially as customers sometimes feel more comfortable ringing to ask for a named individual - you've made it easier for them to react again.

One problem - it all becomes a little confusing if the next three people you employ are all called Rupert!!

It really is a very good discipline to get into the habit of analysing your enquiries each month or even each week if you feel it is necessary. Depending on how often you are advertising you will want to check how a particular advertisement is performing. If you are running a series of advertisements you will want to check how each advert is performing against each other, to spot when the advert needs to be changed or stopped.

Using such a monitoring system will also give you the information you need for future promotions, to be able to predict the levels of response you would expect to generate. Then you can make a more educated judgement regarding the performance of a new advertisement against the old style.

At some stage the advertisements you are running are going to reach their maximum potential as far as enquiry generation is concerned. When that happens, spotting it early can save you valuable resources. You may wish to stop the advert for a while or to change it if you think you can make it more effective.

**Whatever methods of monitoring your advertising you choose, it is important that you identify one individual who will compile the results.** If you leave it to everyone in

your organisation you can be sure that no-one will get on top of it. The person you choose should be able to provide you with a daily, weekly or monthly analysis of the results so that you can plan for the future. To be able to do this, systems need to be put into place so that the correct information is taken over the telephone when customers call and that all the information is directed to the person who is controlling the process. The person responsible should also have the authority to be able to "bully" the other members of staff if vital information such as details of advertising codes are continually missed.

Here's a checklist to follow when starting to advertise:

## CHECKLIST 3 - BOOKING YOUR SPACE

**1**. Have you prepared your advertisement ready for late space?

**2**. Do you have details of the rate card costs to compare with the offers?

**3**. Do you have a budget in mind and a time period during which to spend it?

**4**. Have you set up a bookings number sheet?

**5**. Have you set up a monitoring system?

**6**. Does your advertisement have a code to identify responses?

**7**. Have your staff seen the advertisements and are they aware that they are starting?

*C H A P T E R  6*

# Using advertising features effectively

One of the ways in which you may already have been involved in advertising your company is in a special feature either on yourself or for one of your clients.

Special features are the lifeblood of many papers and magazines. Using features they can create another reason for advertisers to use their product and you'll find that there are a lot of them about. You may already have been approached about putting together your own support feature. They are fairly simple to organise and go something like this:

**1**. You put together a list of your suppliers and pass them to your contact at the paper.

**2**. He or she contacts the list and tries to sell as much advertising to your suppliers as possible.

**3**. The amount of advertising space sold determines the amount of space you will be allocated for the feature. You can use this space for editorial and photographs.

**4**. You generally take a reasonably large ad yourself to increase the size and ensure that the paper can provide you with a good spread in which to promote yourself.

Features are a good way of creating interest, and not just in the initial stages of the business. The fact is that you can use a feature whenever you need to. Anniversaries, moving to new premises, extensions to existing premises, launches of new products and many other reasons are just as good an opportunity to create a feature.

## MAKING A FEATURE A SUCCESS ...

There are a number of things you can do to make sure that a feature is even more effective for your company.

Firstly, if you are in the healthy position of having a couple of good competing newspaper titles to choose from, then you have a good negotiating position and could use it to obtain the best deal for your own advertising. *Maybe the paper will give you a generous discount for letting them run the feature exclusively?*

You have other options though too. You may decide that you would like a feature to appear in more than one paper to maximise coverage. If that's the case, then you could take the decision to simply split your suppliers between the two papers and run two separate features.

Amongst your suppliers there will be those that you feel will support you well and those who you are not sure of, so if you do decide to split your contacts don't give all the main suppliers to one paper and the rest to another because you'll simply finish up with a strong feature in one paper and a weak promotion in the other. Make sure that you allocate them evenly.

*Action Point*

One of the most useful databases to build is a "Suppliers" list which will enable you to contact your suppliers quickly if you need their help. Apart from your normal contact at the supplier, it is also useful to list the Marketing Manager or other contact who may be responsible for making decisions regarding support.

*Sometimes the advertising costs can be prohibitive for your suppliers.* If you are in a position to do a deal, you may wish to negotiate all round discounts to attract more support advertising rather than just keeping the discount for yourself.

Now to the nuts and bolts of putting a feature together and getting the maximum coverage for your company.

After you have decided where to place the feature and hopefully negotiated a reasonable deal, the suppliers will need to be contacted to ask for their support. There are two ways to do this. The first is to list the suppliers and let your contact at the publication sell the space. The second method, which I favour and would recommend, is to have some input yourself at the point of contact with your supplier.

Let's face it, for many companies being asked to support a supplier feature isn't always the way they would prefer to spend their budget. There are times when I have been contacted to advertise in support of a company and I really haven't felt as though I have wanted to, but have felt obliged to. That's how some of your suppliers will feel. I will talk shortly about how your suppliers can get more out of the feature themselves, but for now let's assume that some of your suppliers are not necessarily wildly enthusiastic about supporting you.

## MAKING IT HARDER TO SAY "NO THANKS" ...

If a third party, your contact at the publication, gets in touch with your suppliers without you even having broached the subject it is so much easier for them to say *"I'd love to but I can't"*. That's why I would always write to them personally to ask them for their support first, so at least you've been in touch. The letter can be quite simple but should include a number of important points. They are:

1. Mention why you are running the feature, i.e. that you are using this as part of an ongoing marketing effort.

2. Tell them where the feature is going to be run and the reason for choosing that particular paper, i.e. that it is a strong publication and you are convinced it will help generate many enquiries and sales of their products.

3. Mention the name of the person who will be contacting them on your behalf.

4. Thank them for their support in the past and hope that they will be able to be a part of this important marketing initiative.

Also in the letter, try to emphasise that this is an opportunity for them to sell their products. This is a very important point as I often feel that companies switch off their selling skills when asked to support one of their customers.

For example, how many times have you seen a company with specific products run a **"we are pleased to support J Bloggs"** advertisement in a feature. The supporting company is certainly fulfilling their obligation but doing little more. The point is that if you have a page full of *"we are pleased to support"* advertisements on your feature, it isn't going to help you generate more enquiries for specific products and to sell more of those items.

Make sure that the supporting company understands that you would much rather them place a powerful product advert than a weak support ad. This is, of course, going to be of far more benefit to the supporting company too, so everyone wins.

*One point though.* **Make sure that the supporting company includes your name, address and telephone number on the advertisement, so you receive the enquiries directly.** A product advertisement, no matter how strong, with contact details 200 miles away isn't going to generate too many direct contacts from the local press. But, with your own details inserted, emphasising the local supply angle, the outlook is more promising.

## GETTING EVEN MORE FROM THE PROMOTION...

*Can you do any more to make the feature effective?*

Yes you can. If you have the time to spare you may consider contacting the companies directly yourself to gain more support, or you could delegate the task to someone else in your organisation, as long as they have had contact with the suppliers before. It may be that you would want different people to contact different suppliers, not necessarily to sell them the space on the page but simply to get their agreement to go ahead, then to pass their details onto the paper.

Without doubt you will be able to generate more support than the advertising representative. You have to decide just how important the feature is to you and how much time you wish to allocate to it.

You may wish to target your more important suppliers yourself and leave the rest to the advertisement salesperson. **Whichever way you choose to go, give yourself plenty of time**. Do not be rushed into a decision by the advertising salesperson as it can take a fair while to produce a feature properly. Seven days simply isn't enough time. You will need at least four weeks to build an effective feature.

Remember also that you are still buying advertising space, so the same rules apply regarding positions. Make sure you get a commitment on a position in the paper before you go ahead. Sometimes features are used as fillers and you don't want to be tucked away in the back of the paper after you have spent so long putting it together. **So, as before, an early right hand page will do nicely!**

Unless you are intending to do all the contact work yourself, at some point in time the advertising salesperson is going to be in touch with your suppliers. You can help the representative by not only giving them a list of the companies, the correct contact person and the correct telephone and fax numbers, but also by giving them an idea of what each company supplies to you and highlighting the major companies that you would expect to support you.

That simple information will make their job so much easier as they will be able to relate the products supplied to the local area, giving them an even better chance of making a sale for you. They will also be able to target the main suppliers first, hopefully filling up a page or two quickly. By making their job so much easier, you will be building a great relationship.

And talking of relationships, make sure that you let the salesperson know that you don't want your suppliers put under any pressure - it just isn't worth it. In the past I have had salespeople inferring to me that if I didn't support the company concerned they may even look elsewhere for their supplies. Now, even though I knew that wasn't the case, it seemed to me a needless thing to say and even though the salesperson was nothing to do with the company, it leaves a bad taste in the mouth all the same. Whether you like it or not, as soon as your contact at the paper picks up the 'phone to one of your suppliers, he is representing your company, so be careful to set the ground rules clearly at the start.

Another favourite is *"Well, I do have to make a note of why you don't want to support company X so that they can be given a report"*. Again, this is a needless act of pressure which does no-one any favours, so make sure that the representative you are using to put your feature together understands that if a supplier declines to support you it isn't the end of the world.

When all the advertising has been secured and you are ready to go, you will have to decide how to fill the space you have been allocated. You will generally be offered the services of a reporter to write an article for you which will help you a great deal. However, you should still prepare and make sure that what is written is what you want the readers to see. Make notes about what you would like to get over in the space and explain this to the writer, asking to see a proof copy before it goes to press.

To jazz up a feature even further you might consider running a competition if it is appropriate and, even better, getting a prize from one of your suppliers so that it doesn't cost you anything to run!

Once all the elements are in place it is up to the designers to come up with a powerful design that will get you noticed. Once again, try to keep on top of the feature at this stage and ask to see a visual of how it will appear. If you don't feel that they have done you justice, then

*Quick Tip*

If you think that the feature you are running is going to be a success, you could arrange with the newspaper to print extra copies at the same time as the paper is printed, or alternatively, arrange for extra copies of the paper to be delivered to you. Then you will have a stock of useful promotional literature.

ask them to change the layout. Going right back to when we talked about headlines, be careful that you don't end up with just your company name as the headline which might not mean too much to the readers. Get some creativity into the banner headline and make it jump out of the page.

Just as you should when you are running a series of advertisements, make sure that your staff know the feature is running and show them a copy before the insertion date if you can. There may be support advertising on the page from companies with products that are unfamiliar to them and so they will need to have some information before the 'phones start ringing.

*After the feature has run, what is there left to do?*

Hopefully you will have seen an increase in business and generated some useful enquiries. It's always nice to write to the advertisers who supported you, building on your relationship. They should have received a copy of the feature from the publication, but check just in case and if they haven't had one, get them one. If you are working in a larger company, copy the feature onto the noticeboards so that those colleagues who might not have received the paper get to see it too. This emphasises that the company is active in promoting itself and is good for morale.

**Finally, if you have had a successful feature, why not use it in other ways**? You should be able to get your hands on the artwork and either photocopy or print extra copies to use as you wish. Features are usually one page or more and so are quite powerful. You can use it in the future as part of information packs, introductory letters and in many, many other ways.

Maybe you don't want to go the whole hog right now and have a full suppliers feature, or maybe you have run a feature only a few months ago. If that is the case what else can you do to increase the amount of exposure you are getting in your targeted media?

One method is to negotiate a deal for a set amount of space, i.e. a half or full page, and then sell part of that space off to your suppliers or anyone else that you think might be interested in taking it. Your advertisement is called the *"anchor"* advert and, of course, it is in the best position on the page. You can even create your own features on various topics, knowing that your advertisement is going to be the most powerful on the page. This way you only have to have a couple of contacts to work with to get the idea up and running.

If you want to create the same impact as a feature, with both advertising and editorial support too, you can do so with your own *"Advertorial"*. This type of advertisement has become more popular over the years and can be very effective. Essentially, all you are doing is using the advert space and replacing part of it with an editorial style, so the editorial is seen to be supporting the advertising.

Advertorials tend to work better with larger spaces, and, once again, you can have them prepared and ready for late space offers if you wish. One method of making the Advertorial even more effective is to get the editorial set in the same typeface style as the media you are using. Obviously, if you are going for a late space option in a number of titles this isn't going to be easy, unless they all use the same typeface or you choose to produce a number of alternatives for each title. However, if you are targeting just one title you can easily find out what the typestyle is for both headlines and editorial and match it as closely as you can. The effect is to blend the advert into the paper or magazine and the result is to create something which looks more as if the editorial has been written by the paper and not by yourself.

You may find that the paper will want to place the word *"Advertisement"* above the ad most times. However, if you can get your contact at the publication to forget to do this, then the effect is even better!!

## WHEN THE BOOT IS ON THE OTHER FOOT ...

At some point in the future you may be contacted to support another company in a feature.

*Action Point*

Following a feature you may wish to consider running an advert for a couple of weeks afterwards to strengthen the awareness of your business. You may be able to negotiate a good deal on the space if you combine it with the feature.

As I have already mentioned, unless you have a specific budget for support features, then each time that you get contacted you are going to wish you could get away with as little expenditure as possible.

**The first rule is to treat your advertising in just the same way as if you were advertising in a publication that you have picked for yourself, so none of this "we are pleased to support" stuff.** Make your advertising work for you even if it is being placed in a publication that you feel won't bring you too much business … you never know.

Make sure that you highlight the product or service benefits as we have mentioned earlier. For example, if you are a builder and have been approached to support a feature on a new hospital you have worked on, then one angle would be to promote the reason why you were chosen for the job. Your advertisement might read:

### LOOKING FOR A BUILDER?

### NEED THE JOB TO BE COMPLETED ON TIME?

### HOPING FOR A COMPETITIVE QUOTE?

### TO FIND OUT WHY HOSPITAL X CHOSE BLOGGS & SON TELEPHONE…

*Quick Tip*

In the same way as you may wish to allocate an advertising budget, if you are having to support other companies in features on a regular basis, determining a separate budget for "support" will give you some guidelines to work to and mean that you are less likely to overspend.

You'll also want to make sure that you are taking the smallest space possible that will still give you an effective advertisement. If you are receiving a number of calls for support advertising, then it might be well worth your while settling on a house style for the support ad and producing it in sufficient quantities to see you through the next few months. The cost will be very little compared to the cost of putting an advertisement together time after time.

If you can't afford to contribute to a feature in support of a company, don't feel too badly about it. Generally only a small proportion of those contacted take up the offer. However, to ensure good relations with the featured company, just take the time out to telephone your contact there and let them know that you would have liked to support them but … and if the feature is for an anniversary or an opening, why not send a small card to wish them luck, or even some flowers which will be appreciated by all their staff.

Finally on features, here's a way out that is often available, mainly due to the pressure to run a feature too quickly. Often when you are contacted by a newspaper or magazine to support in a feature, the copy deadline is almost right away. If you can't do the feature, or you don't want to for some reason, then here's a golden opportunity to say no nicely.

*"I'm very sorry, but that just doesn't give me the time to put together the right advertisement. Maybe you can come back to me again if you repeat the feature and give me more time."*

CHAPTER 7
# Where not to advertise

So far we have highlighted where to place your advertising and how to go about it. This short section deals with where it might be wise not to spend your money.

*Generally I'm not too keen on directories, handbooks or similar publications.* I'm not talking about National Telephone Directories which I have found to be effective for almost all the companies I have worked with. I am talking about trade directories and handbooks.

Look around your office. How many *"directories"* or *"handbooks"* do you have on your shelves? How often do you read them, or even use them occasionally to look something up?

I maintain that it isn't very often for most people. In fact, after you have received the publication and glanced at it for a few minutes, making a mental note to take a longer look when you have the time, you have probably filed it away and not touched it since. Years later, when you are going through your files, you decide to throw it out.

**And if you are doing that, what do you think the recipients of the directory in which your advertising appears are doing?**

You can, of course, check. Simply ask the directory salesperson who is the target market - who is going to receive a copy. When you have this information you can call one of them and have a chat about the directory. **Do they use it?** Would they be interested in it? Do they ever look at it or does it get *"binned"* as soon as they receive it? Even if it is a new directory, you can still call a couple of contacts who are *"targets"* and ask them if they feel there is a need for the type of publication on offer.

Directory advertising can be very expensive with companies basing their rates on the fact that the book is going to be *"around"* for a long time. That's fine if the directory is used, but if it isn't, then it could be *"around"* for the next 100 years and it still wouldn't be doing you any good. Take your time and try to be as sure as you can that the money you are spending is being spent for the right reasons and not just because it is easy to book space in a directory each year and forget about it until it's time to book again!

Don't get me wrong, there are some very good directories produced with some excellent information contained in them. However, for the smaller company where budgets are tight, they might not offer the best possible value for money when all things are considered.

If you are doing a lot of *"directory"* advertising, I would suggest you take a long hard look at the leads generated from those publications and then make a decision for the following year. Once again, it emphasises the importance of running an effective monitoring system so that you are basing your spending on hard facts and not just on what you feel might be right at the time. *Advertising in a directory for the seventh year running just because you have been in for the previous six isn't exactly the most convincing reason to go ahead!*

Some time ago we mentioned *"corporate"* style advertising, when a company promotes their name and service rather than specific products. Maybe this type of advertising is more effective in directories, creating an image and building awareness. To be able to afford such advertising you need to be able to allocate a suitable budget which you will accept may not provide you with specific results. If you cannot afford to do this, then don't attempt to style your advertising in this way.

If you are doing directory type advertising, the same rules apply for positions, in fact even more so. The chances are that if you have a new directory land on your desk and you pick it up to look at for the first, and possibly only time, you may only get as far as page 6 or 7 before you are interrupted either by a phone call or by someone entering your office for a chat. **It's very important if you are taking space in directories to get as close to the front as possible if you want to make an impact and, if you can, with a right hand page booking as before.**

Back pages and inside front pages usually carry premiums, but if you are determined to be in the publication you may as well spend a little more to make the advertisement effective. Alarm bells really ring for me when I hear that the directory has **"480" pages**. Believe you me, your advertisement can get really lost in a directory that size! **Having an advertisement on page 176 of a large directory could result in a total waste of your money, so beware.**

Coupons aren't so effective in a directory, simply because people don't like cutting up books and better quality publications which is what a directory generally looks like. Also, there may be some information on the page overleaf that readers do not want to destroy. Think about making the telephone number the main response mechanism in any directory you use and make it as strong as possible.

Directories can be very useful to you in other ways though. Whenever you receive a directory of any kind, look through it to decide whether you have been sent a free mailing list! Make full use of the lists that you will find by using a direct mailing approach, which we will be covering later in the book. In the same way, whenever you are asked to decide about advertising in a directory make sure that you get a copy of last year's to look at. You will need to see the directory to make a proper decision anyway, but, at the same time, you may get another free mailing list too.

These days there are so many choices for your advertising that it is inevitable that you are going to place ads in some media which will not produce you the results you were looking for. As with most things, the golden rule is to learn from your mistakes and not repeat the insertions in the same publication a year later or different publications which are being read *(or not read)* by the same people.

Treat the buying of your advertising in the same way that you would treat the buying of any other important product for your business. Unfortunately, some businesses feel that they have done the hard work when they have set aside a budget for their advertising. In some cases thousands of pounds are spent without ever having an idea of the results. **My advice would be to make whoever is spending your money accountable and to have good reasons for any advertising placed.** That way you stand a chance of making your promotions effective and being in a position to allocate larger funds safe in the knowledge that you are basing your decisions on sound information.

*C H A P T E R   8*
# Getting extra value from your advertising spend

Unless all your advertising design is being done for free, every time you put together a new advertisement you are bound to incur costs for artwork, design or bromides.

If you have an advertisement that you are happy with, it would make sense to use it in other ways which could help to generate new business. **If you send invoices, for example, you could copy the ad and add it to the envelope**. This not only helps to build awareness of your company or products, but also ensures that you are continuing to build a relationship with your customer and gives you the opportunity of creating added sales which you might not have received. We will be discussing later in more depth why it is important to maintain a relationship with an existing customer.

You can also make use of an advertisement by turning it into a leaflet. If you are selling

*Action Point*

If you are advertising in directories of any kind, make a point of reviewing their effectiveness by trying to establish their lead generation record. Make a promise to yourself not to continue with the advertising until are sure it is working for you. At the same time, take a critical look at the advert you are running in the directory. Is it powerful enough to produce results? Is it in the best position, or is it lost, never to be seen? Does it carry a code to identify it for monitoring purposes?

into a market where it is important to get a large amount of information out and about, then this is an ideal method while, at the same time, saving on the creative costs. An added advantage when you follow this route is that you will start to strengthen your message with the advertisement and the leaflet working together. Remember, each time a customer sees the message it goes further and further into their memory, so try to keep the message the same on the various promotions you use.

The message is - don't miss an opportunity to make the most of what is sometimes the costliest element of your budget - the creative component.

## AND, TALKING OF COSTS ...

There is no doubt that using a marketing professional or an Advertising Agency can make a real difference to your creative approach, which, in turn, can make a real difference to your business - *but, can you afford to use one?*

Probably not, which is one of the reasons that you are reading this book.

Choosing and using professionals can be a minefield in itself. Many smaller companies have been disappointed with the results when they have used someone who is supposed to be a *"specialist"*. Many more have been shocked by the cost. Obviously, you need to be sure about the cost implications before work commences, as things can start to run away with themselves if you aren't careful. You also need to realise that a marketing professional or your Ad Agency contact isn't superman and can't *"magic"* results.

The real problem, though, occurs when you are shocked with the costs after the work has been completed. How can you be sure that you are getting value for money and that you won't be facing an embarrassment when the invoice finally arrives on your desk?

Much of the problem arises from a lack of proper briefing. Quite simply, if you have no idea of what you would like to achieve and how you would like to achieve it, you are in danger of opening the floodgates as far as costs are concerned. Whatever you do, get an idea of costs before you agree to start. After all, I would doubt whether you would order a car or a new computer without first getting a quote, so treat your creative work in exactly the same way. If nothing else, place a top limit on the amount that you are willing to spend - *at least that gives some guidelines to work within.*

The more you ask to be done, the more it will cost - it may seem so simple, but sometimes people forget. If you want to see 12 different ad designs, then you'll get charged for 12 separate visuals, even before the first piece of artwork has been produced.

If you are working with an Agency who have much larger clients, for example, they may assume that they would need to produce a number of different ideas for you. If you don't wish to incur the cost, then let them know that two ideas would be fine. If you are reasonably good at understanding what a rough drawing will look like when produced properly, then you can save further by making sure that each of the visuals produced are drawn as roughs and not to a more finished stage. The difference in cost of a full colour visual produced almost to artwork quality and a rough drawing can be very significant indeed, and, if you decide not to use it, a complete waste.

Choosing the right person or company to work with can be difficult too. Sometimes the first contact will have come from the Agency itself who will be eager to gain your business. They may have seen some of your advertising or maybe noticed your company at an exhibition.

There are a number of points to keep in mind when you are trying to decide whether a particular company is the right one for you. Included in them are:

**A.** Do you like the person you will be dealing with? Do you get on well with them at meetings? You'll need to or else the relationship will be over before the start.

**B.** Does either your contact or the company have any specific experience of your products or industry? Have they worked with businesses similar to your own? If not, you

DO YOU LIKE
THE PERSON
YOU ARE
DEALING WITH?

may well be paying for them to learn all about your market for much of the first period.

**C.** Do you like their creative style and will it work well with your products? If you don't like their work, however they try to please you will be in vain.

**D.** Are they close enough to you to be able to make the relationship work and to be handy enough for you both to visit each other on a reasonably regular basis? Travelling across the country may be fun for the first couple of meetings, but becomes a bit of a bore when you have to get up at 5am every time you need to see them. If they come to you it'll cost you an arm and a leg.

**E.** Are their costs reasonable and can you afford them? It's horses for courses, so if they are too rich for your tastes, don't get involved since even the simplest job will be too expensive for you.

**F.** Are their existing customers from companies your own size? Are they happy with the work and the charges? If they have a client list full of multi-nationals, it will be unlikely that they will suit your needs - at least not for a few years yet!!

Choosing a professional to work with is as difficult as choosing a new employee. Unless you know them well, really well, you can't be sure just how it's going to work out. As you do sometimes with a new employee, you may wish to consider a trial period where you can both get to know each other first. Better to find out after a couple of months that you've made a mistake, than to struggle for years with a relationship which just isn't going to work.

Costs of a number of items will give you a clue as to just how expensive the agency is. They should be able to give you an indication of an hourly rate for artwork along with a cost for an A4 full colour visual. Obviously it will only be an estimate, but it may point you in the right direction.

You can also ask the new company to quote for a job that you have already had produced and compare prices. **Bear in mind though that the first price you receive from a company keen to do business with you can sometimes be the lowest!**

Very often, getting the most from the marketing budget is very much about using different companies for different projects. The printer that is giving you the best deals for the smaller jobs probably won't be the best to deal with for something bigger. It's a question of picking and choosing as you go along. One thing's for sure though. If you are doing a lot of different print jobs and you are using just one printer you probably aren't getting the best deals that you could. In fact the printer you are using may well be sub-contracting some of the work which they can't handle.

If you are new to the game, then being a member of the local Business Club can really prove to be useful. The contacts you'll pick up at the meetings will be very valuable and could end up saving you a deal of money. Asking other companies who they use for certain jobs is the easiest method of tapping into the professionals in any area.

Getting your artwork produced through a printer can also be cost effective. They have a number of contacts with a whole range of artists and typesetters and you could do worse than ask them for their advice.

In the end, the decision to use an outside agency or a marketing professional to help you grow the business is one that only you can take. If you are struggling to make an impression in a market and you don't feel that you have the skills to make a difference quickly enough, then it could be wise to look at using a specialist in the same way that you would use an accountant or solicitor.

Maybe you do have the ideas to help you develop, but you are just too tired at the end of the day to be able to put them into action. If this is the case, having a professional guide you without having to employ another person might just be the move that makes your business grow even faster.

---

## Summary Points

1. Think about your target market and make sure that you know exactly who you need to be "talking to".

2. Don't commit yourself to advertising until you are absolutely ready.

3. Consider asking your customers what they read to pinpoint the correct media for you.

4. Spend time producing your advertisement. Remember to follow the simple guidelines which can make your campaign more effective.

5. Allocate a budget for your advertising so that you aren't tempted to spend more than you can afford.

6. Build a relationship with your contacts at the paper or magazine.

7. Always try to get the best possible position for your advertising.

8. Keep a check on the prices you are paying to ensure that you are getting the best deals. Always ask for discounts.

9. Put into place an effective monitoring system before you start to spend money.

10. Review your results constantly. If it's not working stop it as soon as possible.

11. Always make your advertising work for you, even when supporting another company on a feature.

12. Be careful not to spend money in areas which will not be cost effective for you. Never advertise without a good reason to do so.

*SECTION TWO*
# Public Relations

*C H A P T E R   1*

# Learning to make PR a cost-effective part of your marketing report

When people think of public relations, or PR as it is generally known, they tend to imagine beautiful girls draped over a gleaming car or boat, or, worse still, the heavy drinking *"PR Man"* leaning across the bar buying yet another round of gin and tonics.

Of course, it happens. But you probably don't sell the type of product that you could drape a leggy blonde over and, like myself, you're probably happier with a pint of beer than a gin and tonic.

Incorporating the use of public relations into your own marketing plan needn't be an expensive option. The exciting fact is that public relations can be used effectively by even the smallest business. It can be a very low cost method of building awareness of your products, raising the profile of your company and, last but certainly not least, generating low cost leads.

**And you don't have to be an expert in PR to make it work.** In its very simplest form PR is about creating a press release that will be used in a newspaper or a trade magazine. This isn't as difficult as it may sound. Securing PR coverage in the papers or magazines in which you would normally consider advertising can be very rewarding in terms of numbers of enquiries generated. Readers react well to an effective press release and, on many occasions, you may well find it out-performing a paid-for advertisement, making the use of PR very attractive to all types of companies and especially so to smaller companies with more limited budgets.

*Getting a press release carried by a paper can be remarkably easy.* Media of all types are always on the lookout for material to fill their space. Journalists are just as lazy as the rest of us at heart and if you can provide them with material to fill a page, they will certainly consider using it.

In any business, large or small, there is always news of some sort happening. Just think of the possibilities:

A new product

An anniversary

A new member of the team

An extension to the premises

An unusual use of one of your products

Your first customer

Your thousandth customer

An unusual customer

A large order

*The list is endless.*

## HOW TO GET STARTED ...

You could simply telephone your local paper and ask to speak to the newsdesk, giving them the details of your news. However, this way you are leaving a lot to chance. You may find that by putting in a little extra effort, you have greater success. Even if your story is only suitable for the local press, the best option will be to present the details in writing and to send a full press release to the paper - *and then follow it up.*

The most effective method is to make contact with the correct reporter first, find out exactly what details they may be interested in, then send in your news release, following it up a few days later to make sure it has been received and understood. Following up your releases whenever possible and building a relationship with the editor or reporter are very important. PR is a people business and so working on building relationships will almost certainly produce results.

*Let's assume that you have a newsworthy story.* Being newsworthy is very important. It's hard work if you send in a release that has very little real news value at all. Even worse, if you continue to send releases that are really just advertisements in a different form then the paper will soon begin to ignore you and may miss the one release you send of any real value. It's very simple really: the more news in your release, the more chance you have of getting it used.

Having said that, if you follow a programme of product linked press releases, even the smallest change to the product specification may be enough to hang a release around. Something that you may take for granted, such as a model being available in an extra size for example, may be deemed to be worthy of space in a trade magazine, especially one that is struggling to fill its quota of editorial that particular month !

**A press release is not an advertisement.** The press release should be written in a softer, more informative way. For example, if you were promoting a new type of knife and in your advertising you boast that "The Quickslice is guaranteed to outperform all its rivals", when writing a press release you would take a more informative view and say something like " The new Quickslice has performed very well in trials and its manufacturers are confident that users will enjoy the benefits of its unique design."

When you make the decision to send a press release to a paper or magazine, the very first thing to do with your blank piece of paper is to head it *"Press Release"*. This may sound a little obvious, but if you don't identify exactly what you are sending your work could well end up on the wrong desk or, even worse, in the bin. If you have gone to the trouble of writing a press release, then at least make sure it gets to the right person.

If you feel that a PR approach may suit your company and you intend to use it extensively in the future, it may be worth getting some special Press Release letterheads printed which will both catch the eye and help to build awareness of your company name. Just as you would want to create an impact with your product literature when it is first seen by the customer, it is just as important to try to ensure that your release stands out from the crowd on what may be a pretty packed editor's desk. However, initially it is reasonably effective to use your own letterheads and to strip *"Press Release"* across the top of the page - big and bold.

Below the *"Press Release"* heading you will want to use a title for the release. Here's an opportunity to really grab the attention of the journalist. If you create a really eye-catching heading, not only has it got more chance of being read but that headline may be used in the paper. If you aren't that creative, don't worry, just go for a simple line such as **"New Product from XXXXX is sure to make life easier"**.

Your press release should be **typed and double-spaced.** This makes it easier for the journalist to read and to make notes on if they wish. The length of the release is really up to you, but you may want to consider that shorter releases have more chance of being used rather

**NOTES**

*Quick Tip*

Whenever you have the opportunity to place a press release along with an advertisement on a feature, request that the release be given the "first on the piece" position, so that your details are the first ones to be read on the page. Positions for press release material is just as important as positions for adverts.

than a four or five page effort which may be difficult to edit. All papers and magazines need fillers and if that's what your release is used for - great, it's still in the paper and doing the job that you intended it to do.

Of course, I should point out that you don't necessarily have to do the work yourself. When you have a particularly good story which you think will create some interest, then why not try to get the newspaper or magazine to send a reporter to write the story for you. If you do follow this course, then try to make sure that you get to see the editorial before it is used. The problem with leaving the job to a third party is that sometimes the result isn't quite as you envisaged and the important points that you wanted to see emphasised are missed. At least if you have written the piece yourself, you can be reasonably confident that there will be few misquotes and errors to product names etc.

Putting your own press releases together gives you more control and allows you to spread the news more widely. If a particular title writes and carries a story, then other competitive magazines or papers may not feel as though they want to carry it too, especially if they only get hold of it a week or so later.

Ideally, if you have the time and feel comfortable generating your own PR, you should try to create a bank of press releases for general use whenever you need them. When you are asked to advertise in a feature, for example, one of the questions you should be asking is *"can I provide some editorial?"*. This is far easier to do if you already have the press release prepared.

Press releases of various lengths about various product ranges or services that you offer will be worth their weight in gold, so do consider building a small reserve of them yourself. Even if you are booking deadline advertising space, if you have press material handy, you may still be able to sneak in the odd release which will both strengthen your advert and give you another opportunity to generate enquiries.

*Action Point*

After you have written a press release, make a number of copies and place them in a file ready for when you need the information quickly. Always ask whether you can send in some PR along with any ads you might be booking. You'll be surprised how many papers and magazines will say yes !

*CHAPTER    2*

# Writing a press release that will get used

As we have said, writing a press release is a little different than writing an advertisement. Basically you don't have to be quite so clever when writing a press release as you may have to be when trying to sell your product in an advert. You may be surprised how easy it can be to put together your own press release.

There are some very simple rules to remember when writing your release. They are

**What, Who, Where, When, Why and How.**

If you ask yourself these questions about your product, service or other subject you may be writing about, you will be able to work your information around this framework.

*Let's look at a simple example.* Company X have a new kettle which they are launching at an exhibition. A short release could be written like this:

### *PRESS RELEASE...PRESS RELEASE...PRESS RELEASE...*

### *SALES OF NEW KETTLE COMING TO THE BOIL*

A new kettle, which is claimed to bring water to the boil quicker and save on electricity bills, has just been launched at the major hardware exhibition by Cambridge company Kettle Kings Ltd.,

Using the latest technology, it is claimed that the "Quicky Kettle" will make a real difference in the kitchen, saving valuable minutes for all the family.

John Bloggs, Marketing Director for Kettle Kings, is sure that the new kettle is a winner. "Trials have shown it to be very popular because of its boiling speed," said John. "We expect the kettle to be amongst the best sellers very shortly."

Kettle Kings are just two years old, but have already reached an impressive turnover and are looking to expand further.

Details of the "Quicky" are available from the company by telephoning ——— or writing to ——— etc. etc.

**ENDS**

For further information call John Bloggs, Marketing Director on ———

**EDITOR'S NOTES**

1. Kettle Kings are a British owned company and employ 32 people at present.

2. Kettle Kings are funding expansion plans with a development grant valued at £350,000.

3. The "Quicky" is the second new product to by developed be Kettle Kings following the success of the "Mini Kettle" earlier this year.

So there you have it - a simple press release. We can now run through the release and explain the various elements.

*First the six questions we listed:*

**What** - The "Quicky" Kettle

**Who** - Kettle Kings

**Where** - From Cambridge

**When** - At the hardware show

**Why** - Because the kettle boils more quickly

**How** - Get details from the company

The press release has been written with short paragraphs to make it easier for the reader and for the journalist who will be deciding whether to use it. *Short paragraphs mean that it will be easier to edit too.* The first paragraph should set the scene and leave the reader in no doubt what you are going to tell them. Just like the headline in an advertisement, the first few lines are so important to get the attention of both the journalist and the reader when it finally manages to make it into a paper or magazine. It is the first few lines which will determine whether your release catches the attention of the journalist, so make them interesting.

Obviously, the Kettle King company will be hoping that anyone looking for a new kettle will be interested in their news and so they could have taken a different angle and actually tailored it to target their potential market even more closely by stating:

**"Anyone interested in a new, faster, more efficient kettle will be interested in the new Quicky Kettle, launched recently by Kettle Kings."**

They could even have highlighted the problem of older kettles:

**"If your kettle takes an age to come to the boil, you are sure to be interested in the new Quicky, a recent development from Kettle Kings."**

The second paragraph fills in the details a little more and emphasises the main selling point. However, it doesn't make wild exaggerated claims for the product. In a press release you may have to tone down the sales talk otherwise it may not get printed. The golden rule is to stick to the facts and if the facts are a little unbelievable, then add some details to back up your claims in the editor's notes which we will come to in a moment.

Comments from a member of staff or, even better, a customer, are very valuable if you can work one into the release. Once again, make the quote believable. Any other information about the product or company can be used to complete the story along with another call to action, just like we should be using in our advertising.

Sometimes the call to action in a press release will be removed if the media feel that it is too *"commercial"*. Try to keep it as general as possible. In a press release, if the customer has read the information, you shouldn't have to be so pushy. On the majority of occasions your telephone and address details will be included and that's the trigger for the enquiries to roll in. **Remember, they are all virtually free and well worth having!**

At the end of the press release simply add the word *"ENDS"* in block capitals. This lets the journalist know that the press release has finished and that the additional information on the page is only for them - background details which can be used for further column inches if they need more. If you forget to insert *"ENDS"* and then put your own personal contact name and number, don't be surprised to see it included in the story when it appears in the paper - a touch inconvenient if you have given your home number and you are besieged with calls every day for a week.

The editor's notes should give whoever is dealing with your release some background information to strengthen your story or to make them more familiar with your company. It may be the trigger to get them more interested and the reason they end up producing a full page profile on you, so it is important if you can to create a few interesting notes. Details of your history, growth and any expansion plans are the sort of things to include.

"*CONGRATULATIONS! YOU'RE OUR 1000th CUSTOMER!*"

## CHECKLIST NO. 4 - WRITING A PRESS RELEASE

1. Have you identified your work as a press release at the top of the page?

2. Have you covered the What, Who, Where, When, Why & How elements?

3. Do you have a snappy headline?

4. Does your first paragraph catch the imagination and make sure the reader knows what you are going to tell them?

5. Have you been able to include a comment or testimonial?

6. Have you added a call to action?

7. Are your sentences and paragraphs short and easy to read?

8. Have you used double-spacing?

9. Have you included an "ENDS"?

10. Have you produced some editor's notes?

## CHAPTER 3
# Getting the most from PR

Unfortunately there's no easy way of ensuring that your press release will be used. When you are successful it is known as *"landing"*, but if your release doesn't *"land"*, don't be despondent - it may take some time.

It may be worth talking to the contacts at the various media to ask them why they didn't use your release. This way you can be sure that the details you sent were presented in the correct way. You may find out that they would have preferred a different approach, in which case you will know for the future. While you are asking their advice, of course, you can tell them all about your company, products or service and get them more interested in you. Calling someone for their advice always gives them a bit of a buzz, so use it to your best advantage.

**Just as in direct mail, the target list is very important.** In PR the contacts you have at the media are key, especially if you have a strong relationship with them. If you can get to know some of them, either over the telephone or, even better, face to face, you will see better results from your work. You may even find them calling you for news in the future, which is a very cost effective way to promote yourself.

In the same way that direct mail is effective the more you send, then the same is true with PR. However, beware, as just as there is a limit to the frequency of letters you can send a potential customer before they switch off, so there is a limit to the number of press releases you can send before the journalist switches off. Only send good quality information, not rubbish and only send it when the time is right, not every week come what may.

Talking of timing, knowing the copy deadlines of the media is also important, especially if you are launching a major product and most of the titles you are targeting are monthly or even quarterly publications. If you get the timing wrong, or you are unaware of the deadline and miss it, you could be waiting some time before you get the opportunity to obtain coverage again.

**Some releases can hang around for ages before they are used.** Maybe they haven't quite made it into the issue you targeted and have been put into a *"possibles"* file for the future. It could be months before being used, which is one good reason not to include prices of products on releases unless you feel it is very necessary.

A press release *"landing"* in a publication with an old price included doesn't create the best impression with the customer, especially if they have kept the article and then receive the information with a higher price listed. Prices can be placed in the editor's notes along with an indication to the journalist to check the current price before publication if the information is used after a certain date.

### BRINGING THE PRESS TO YOU...

If you are launching a new product or opening a new shop or factory, you may consider having a *"Press Day"* at your premises. Press days can either work very well or be total flops. Here's a few pointers to try to ensure that your event is worthwhile.

A press event doesn't have to be elaborate, but you should try to make it as professional as possible, so planning is very important. You can either invite the media at a specific time if you are intending to unveil something special or have a grand opening or, alternatively, you could invite them along to an *"open house"* type event and deal with them whenever they turn up. Obviously, if you invite them to come along anytime during the day, they may have more opportunity to get to you, depending on what is happening in the news elsewhere.

You will have to write to your contacts with an invitation. This is where the contact list is so crucial - the quality of the names on your list will be all important for the success of the event. When you write to the contacts, don't give them every single last detail of why you are holding the press event. Hold some of the details back from the information you send. If you

> *Quick Tip*
> Try to keep a record of what releases you have sent to which media, especially if you are rotating your press material. A record of the releases sent and the coverage received will help you to build up a picture of those media using your material and those which don't seem to be interested. You can then tackle the problem areas individually.

> *Quick Tip*
> Always make sure that the press register with you at any event, however small. That way you always have a record of who attended and you can follow them up afterwards. Place a registration book at the entrance, along with your press packs.

**NOTES**

**Action Point**

Building a list of PR contacts on a database will prove to be very useful. Once again, being able to send information quickly and with little effort will give you the edge.

don't, you will have given them all the information that they feel they might need and in the process given them little reason to come along on the day.

Following up after the invites have been sent is very important for this type of event. You should call to make sure that they have received the invitation and to get an idea of whether or not each contact is going to be attending. Much of the time they really will not know because it will depend on what else is going on, but if you can get a commitment, then all the better. If your contact informs you that there is no way that they are going to be able to attend and no-one else can cover for them, make sure you let them know that you will send them full details afterwards and try to get their commitment to use the information that you will be sending to them.

**Timing is also very important too.** As we have already mentioned, deadlines are sometimes crucial and it's wise to know the deadlines of the important contacts you are thinking of inviting. If all the local papers are published on Thursday morning you probably won't want your event on the Wednesday afternoon or the Thursday morning as you will have to wait a whole week before you have an opportunity for your news to be published. Close to deadlines are a bad time to hold events as the journalists are generally running around trying to close an issue. Find out from your contacts the best time for them and the best time to ensure maximum coverage and go from there.

If you are holding a Press Conference, keep it short. Once again, find out what the best time of the day will work for your contacts and go with that. It may be around 10.30-11.00am. Twenty minutes or less for a presentation followed by a short question and answer session is fine. If you have a product that can be demonstrated, then demonstrate it. Remember that journalists need to be sold on the idea too and the more they like what you have the more they are likely to write about it. Try to get them enthusiastic !

Refreshments should be available even if it is just coffee and biscuits and you should try to hold the event in a comfortable room. If you estimate that you will have only six or seven people attending, then don't use a room which can hold 200 as it will look too low key however you try to dress it up. After the presentation and questions you will want to talk to the press individually to pass on any extra information they would like. If you have staff, make sure that one or two of them are there too so that they can support you. However, brief them properly about the message you are trying to get over and what they should be saying (and not saying).

A nice touch if you can arrange it is to have loyal customers, product users or suppliers there too who can also talk to the press. This will add another angle and give the media the opportunity to generate quotes galore. Once again though, choose carefully as they could say anything to the press.

**Quick Tip**

Choosing the right venue for a press conference can be critical. A venue which is well known will attract more people and if you can choose a venue which is in some way connected to the message you are attempting to promote, even better. If you do decide to use an outside venue you may be lucky enough to find professional management who can help you considerably to pull the press. After all, it's in their interests too for you to succeed.

As the visitors arrive you should give them a press pack which will include a press release, any other notes, a photograph, brochures and any other information that you want them to have. **Photographs are important as you may not be lucky enough to get a photographer from the media there on the day.** By giving out your own photographs you can be sure that each of the visitors has access to a shot if they need one.

## SAY CHEESE ...

Whatever event you are running, don't rely on getting a photographer from the papers to attend. If you can, invest in a photographer yourself and you can be safe in the knowledge that at least you'll have some shots of the event at the end of the day. You can always send the photographs to the papers the next day or, if it is really desperate, later that same day. If you do decide to engage a photographer for a couple of hours, make sure you brief them as to what you require. Make a list of the types of photographs you would like and talk it through before the day if possible.

It's a good idea to get the photographer to arrive at least half an hour before the event so that he can get to know the area you are using and any products you are featuring. At the same time they can run through the event again with you. As you may well be running around in circles at this stage, you would do well to brief the photographer even earlier than that - a day or two before if possible.

You will have to decide which shots you need, whether you need them in black and white or colour and whether you would like either colour transparencies, colour prints or both. This is simply a case of sitting down and thinking just how you would use the photographs if you had them. Usually it's best to take both black and white and colour since you never know when you are going to need them in the future. The cost of shooting colour at the same time as black and white or vice versa is very little compared to the additional cost of having to re-shoot some time later.

If you are opening a shop or a factory it is often a nice gesture to arrange for colour prints of your staff or any official who has helped you with the opening. *You can give them away and have them on your walls for posterity.* The extra cost is very little and it's good for team spirit, so don't forget to have a team photo taken before the day begins - another good reason for getting the photographer there earlier rather than later.

A CONTACT SHEET MAKES CHOOSING PHOTOS EASIER AND LESS EXPENSIVE

To ensure that you don't end up with hundreds of photographs that you are never going to use, put limits on the number of shots you want. That way you won't end up with a larger than expected bill. Another way to cut down on the cost is to request a *"Contact Sheet"* after you have had the event. A contact sheet is simply a reference sheet showing you all the black and white shots the photographer has taken in miniature form. It will be useful in the future for you to use to choose other shots that you might need. From the contact sheet you can choose the shots you want and leave the others on file. If you don't ask for a contact sheet the likelihood is that the photographer will automatically send you one of every shot he has taken

*Quick Tip*
If there is a rush for photos, then ask the photographer to choose the best couple of shots to print. At the same time also get a contact sheet so that you can make a more leisurely choice of other shots later. For press work you will usually require either 7" x 5" or 10" x 8" black and white photographs.

*- and that could be a lot of shots !*

Costs can rise when you are printing hundreds of black and white shots. If you think that you are going to require a continuous supply of photographs you may wish to base your decision on which photographer to use partly on his pricelist for additional prints. In other words, check how much the cost per print is before you choose the photographer for the job. Generally, the more you purchase the cheaper the unit cost, but prices do vary, sometimes considerably, so bear it in mind at the outset and you shouldn't get caught.

The photographer will generally keep the black and white negatives which you will order off, but will give you the colour transparencies. He will also keep the negatives from the colour prints if you have had any taken. If you think that you will need a number of colour transparencies to use with the media in the future, then consider asking the photographer to take a number of the same shot while he is on the premises. *It may be less expensive than duplicating them later.* Unfortunately, when you send colour shots to the media, you cannot rely on them sending them back, so if you think that you might need extra photos, request them at the time of the shoot and it will save you money in the long run.

Finally regarding the photographer, if you have anything else you would like a shot of for the future, even a professional family shot, then that's the time to get it and to make the most of your money while he's around!

## PUTTING YOUR PRESS PACK TOGETHER ...

**What do you send out with your press release?** It varies. There's little point in sending a colour transparency to a paper that only prints in black and white. Get to know the media you are targeting as much as you can to find out what they would prefer. In some media it's almost impossible to get a photograph published. In this case send the release on its own or maybe with a photocopy of a photograph. They can then come back to you if they require a shot.

I like to send any available product information along with the press release, for a couple of reasons. Firstly the leaflet or brochure might give additional information which could increase coverage and, secondly, if a brochure includes a number of photographs or illustrations, the journalist may spot a shot that they would like to use. Don't send too much information though - *you don't want to swamp them.*

If you do have colour photographs available, but don't send them with your release, make a point of mentioning the fact in the *"notes"* section. Getting a black and white photo published is good, but getting a colour shot into the press is even better. You may find that the publication will carry a colour shot but at a price. They may well charge to cover *"colour separation"* charges. You will have to decide whether it is worth paying the fee for the additional interest it may generate.

If you do send photographs it is important to ensure that they stay with the release. If they get separated they may not be easy to identify. By following this routine we can ensure that our details are reasonably safe:

A. Type a caption of 20 or 30 words onto the bottom of an A4 piece of paper. Add your contact details.

B. Arrange the photograph onto the A4 sheet and photocopy the photograph onto the sheet with the caption below.

C. Lightly attach the photograph directly onto the photocopy of itself, so that the photograph can be pulled off easily when required.

Using this method, the photograph is attached to the caption sheet. If it accidentally goes missing, then there is still a record of what it is and the caption to identify it. There may be hundreds of photographs in the press office at any one time and so when one goes missing it can be very difficult to match it up to the release unless you take precautions as detailed above.

## OTHER WAYS TO GET YOUR NAME OUT AND ABOUT......

Creating your own press release is an excellent method of increasing the number of enquiries generated. There are other ways of achieving coverage too. For example, if you have a unique product, then you could attempt to get the item tested and a report written by a journalist, just as in the same way cars are test driven and articles written and published.

**Does your target media have product review pages?** If so, arrange to send a product to the journalist responsible to try. Articles written by a third party in a testimonial style are so much more powerful than a news release sent from you yourself ...

*MAKE YOUR PRESS PACK
AS INTERESTING AS POSSIBLE*

> **Quick Tip**
>
> If you are selling through distributors, you can help them by providing them with good press material for them to use locally.

If you attend exhibitions, don't forget to take along press releases for the press room. Some exhibitions won't have this facility, but many will as they rely on the press to cover the show and to build awareness, especially if the show is running for any length of time. If you are launching a new product at the show, then let the Organisers know well beforehand as they may wish to use your product as part of their show promotional activities.

Show Organisers are always keen to receive information that will help them to create interest in the event, especially news of new products that are being seen first at the show, so you may well end up with the Organisers doing your PR for you.

When taking press material to a show, place your releases in clear folders to keep them tidy on the shelf in the press room. Enclosing photographs in the front of the pack adds interest and means, especially in a busy show with a large press room, that the press pack has more chance of catching the eye of the journalist.

Adding a flash to the folder such as *"New Product"* or *"Don't miss this new idea"* can also help. It is important to keep on returning to the press room during the show to make sure that your press releases are in a prominent position. It's the same principle as the chocolate bar salesman who moves his bars to the front of the unit on each visit. It may seem a little over the top, but if it means that your products or your company are featured in a large circulation magazine free of charge as a result, then the effort is well worthwhile I assure you.

**Oh, and don't worry about moving one of your competitor's press releases out of the way and behind another set of information - they are probably doing the same thing to yours!!**

## MEASURING THE RESULTS ...

You will be putting time, effort and some financial resources into a PR campaign and so you will want to know whether it is working for you.

PR leads should be monitored in exactly the same way as advertising enquiries. Sometimes you will be lucky enough to be part of a *"reader response"* mechanism and so you'll find it easy to identify the source of the enquiry, but often there will only be the telephone call or a letter into your company.

You can create your own identification by using a special code as part of your address on your press release or even by using a special name to direct enquiries to. Inserting either of these in the *"call to action"* will give you more control over the responses.

As before, getting your staff to ask the question *"where did you hear about us?"* is the simplest way of ensuring that you can get an idea of the effectiveness of the work you are doing. Sometimes the first indication that you have been featured in a magazine or newspaper will be when you receive the first call or letter from a customer. When this happens, try to get hold of a copy of the page on which you are featured to make sure you know what has been written about you.

PRESS CUTTINGS BOOK

You should keep all your successes in a **press cuttings book.** Your press book should be kept up to date as far as possible so that you have something to show off to visitors, whether they are new suppliers, new customers or even your friendly bank manager. A healthy press cuttings book is a very valuable tool when it comes to convincing potential business colleagues that you are a go-ahead company and it gives a good *"feel"* to the organisation.

No matter how large or small your company, no matter which products or services you are selling, no matter whether you have local or national coverage, there's a place for PR in your promotional plans. Not only that, but you will find, as you develop your programme, that PR can be a most cost effective method of building awareness, creating enquiries and generating sales.

It isn't hard to do, it isn't hard to start, so why not start now?

Oh, and just one more thing - **Never believe your own PR!!**

---

## Summary Points

1. Always try to make your press material "newsworthy". In any business there should always be things happening which are worth reporting.

2. Build up a "bank" of press material if you can, to be able to be used at a moment's notice.

3. If you aren't successful the first time, stick with it. PR can generate you very cost effective leads if handled properly.

4. Produce good quality photographs. A good shot will help the release to get used; a poor photo will hinder its chances.

5. Measure your results in exactly the same way as you would with your advertising.

*SECTION 3*

# Introducing Direct Mail into your business

" I TOLD YOU 2 WEEKS WAS TOO LONG TO BE AWAY ! "

••••••••••••••••••••
**NOTES**

*C H A P T E R   1*
# Understanding the power of Direct Mail

All over the world, every day, more and more unsolicited pieces of mail are landing on doormats in every type of home and office. Whether you live in a block of council flats or a mansion in the country, whether you are working in a small office alone or are a manager in a multi-national company, you can be sure that someone, somewhere, is eager to mail you details about products or services that they think you may be interested in buying.

*So why has the Direct Mail Industry grown so quickly and why will it continue to grow even faster during the next few years?*

**The answer is quite simple - it works.**

That's right, it works to sell products. It works to keep customers and it works to get further information that will make it easier to sell in the future. You can be sure it works for two very simple reasons. Firstly, direct mail is very easily monitored and measured. You send something and you either get a reaction or you don't. You know how many you have sent, to whom and you know what resulted. In short, if it didn't work then millions of companies just wouldn't keep spending millions of pounds mailing and developing new methods to make it work even more effectively.

And the second reason? That's easy. It's a good bet that most of us will have bought something as a result of a direct mail letter sometime in the past.

Yes, like millions of others you will almost certainly have been influenced to make a purchasing decision by information you have been sent. You may not have rushed out immediately to buy a product because of a mailer, but the chances are that it has formed a part of your decision to buy - however small.

*If it is so effective then, why isn't everyone at it?*

Well, there's no real reason that I can see that they shouldn't be. I believe that almost every company, no matter how small or large, no matter what they are selling and to whom, could benefit enormously by making direct mail an important and integral part of their overall marketing effort.

Notice that I said a "part" of the overall marketing effort. I am not suggesting for one moment that everyone should call a halt to their advertising campaigns, stop all public relations work and never go to another exhibition again. Simply that direct mail can be used and, in many cases, should be used alongside other activities to gain new customers and to keep existing ones.

**Keeping customers is so very important.** It is said that finding a new customer costs five times as much as selling again to an old customer. With this in mind, direct mail is one of the best ways to keep in touch with your customer base and to ensure that the next time they want to buy, they come back to you first to give you a chance of supplying them.

Having considered some of the advantages of direct mail, why don't more companies use it more often ? Well, these could be just some of the reasons:

- They are not convinced that a first or second class stamp will be cost effective.

- They don't know whom to mail to.

- They don't know how to produce an effective mailer.

- They haven't the facilities to prepare the mailer.

These are all excuses which could be used for not getting involved with a direct mail programme. Having said that, none of them is such a good reason that, if you have the will to try new things and the desire to see your business develop, you should be held back.

I have been a fan of direct mail for some time. However, a few years ago I experienced something that made me even more aware of its power. With just a name taken from good old Yellow Pages, a simple letter and a second class stamp, my company **gained new business which was worth some £100,000** during the following 12 month period. Now that's cost effective marketing !!

## GETTING STARTED ...

To get started with a direct mail programme you first have to prepare or source a list of potential customers to send your offer to. The first group you may wish to talk to may be your existing customers. This begs the question *"Do you have your customers listed and readily accessible either on computer or a manual system?"*

One of the greatest crimes that you can commit as a businessman must surely be to throw away your customers' names and addresses if you have at some point captured them. You will have worked hard and spent considerable amounts getting them. Discard them as if you had found them lying around and you'll be wasting enormous time and resources - in short you are making hard work of growing your business.

Sometimes, of course, businesses do not know their customers' names and addresses. For example, a greengrocer's would not usually have a mailing list created from the visitors into their shop. However, I would bet that somewhere a progressive greengrocer does have his customers on a mailing list and maybe, twice a year or so, mails them a special offer to bring them back into his shop - just in case they have started to stray.

Don't ever think that you can't get hold of your customers' names and addresses. There are always ways to do it.

If you invoice your customers, then you will already have your mailing list. If you don't already keep records of your past clients then you should start to build a mailing list straight away. It may take a little time to build into a useable system, but, if you don't start somewhere then you'll never be in a position to take advantage of what is a golden opportunity to get ahead of your competition, build customer loyalty and extra ongoing business. Remember that a mailing list can be any size and that even if you are mailing to just a handful of contacts on a regular basis, you will be doing yourself no harm whatsoever.

If you have a retail outlet, where your customers visit you on a fairly frequent basis, are there the same good reasons for putting a direct mail campaign in place? Well, yes, I believe that there are. Whatever type of business you have, can you ever be sure of your customer loyalty? If you can, you must be quite an extraordinary business, because the vast majority of companies have to keep working to maintain loyalty.

Even if you think that you are securing all your customer's business, you can never be totally sure. In reality you are probably sharing your customer with a number of other competing companies.

Worse still, you may have lost a number of customers to a competitor or maybe the customer has simply stopped buying the product you sell - from anybody. Although this may have happened for a number of reasons, the chances are that you will be able to interest the customer once again - *if you can get to them and give them enough encouragement.*

## AN EXAMPLE ...

I am a member of a video club. I'm sure that many of you reading this book are also members of such a club. A local video club is typical of the type of small local retail outlet that could quite easily use direct mail to promote its products more effectively.

*Why?* Well, first of all it has the names and addresses of all its members. Most of them will almost certainly be locals and so mailings could even be hand delivered if necessary to save postage. Secondly, the video club business has new products available all the time with new titles and, thirdly, the video business is typical of the type of business that has different categories of customer.

**This last point is very important.** You see, some of your customers may be the type that need to have a special reason to visit you and buy from you again. Maybe you need to get them excited about what you are selling to bring them back into the fold. You will always be lucky enough to have the very loyal customer who buys regularly and needs very little maintenance, but it is the infrequent customer, the type that drifts in and out of your business, that should be your major concern and primary target.

A good, consistent direct mail programme can influence the drifters to come back into your business. If you can recapture a percentage of your infrequent customers and entice them to spend with you on a more regular basis, your business will automatically grow, just by taking a little more care of this customer group that all too often gets forgotten.

## FINDING THE TRIGGER ...

I am most definitely in the *"infrequent"* customer group for the video club. My family rents videos in spurts, as many families tend to do. It can be seasonal of course, with more interest in videos on the longer and colder winter nights, but it is also down to the *"trigger"* that gets us interested and excited about certain products.

A *"purchase trigger"* is the key that unlocks the sale - in other words, the reason for the customer making the decision to find out more about a particular product. And what is the trigger on this occasion? Yes, of course, it is a new film, just released and available to hire.

So, find the trigger and sales will follow. I can guarantee that if my video shop had sent me details of a few new releases I would have rented more videos from them. Somewhere there would have been a new product that I would have been interested in. But they haven't sent me any information and I haven't given them any business for quite a while. There are thousands of businesses losing sales just like the video shop because they are taking a passive approach to their market place and towards their existing customers.

When you think about it logically it really does make sense. I am a customer of the video shop. That means I have rented videos in the past. I enjoy renting videos when I find something I would like to view. The shop's problem, or opportunity, is that I don't tend to rent many products from them during the course of the year. However, the bottom line is that I am a buyer and so if you put more similar products in front of me the chances are that I will buy again. I am a warm target. I am a better bet than someone who hasn't used the service before.

Sending details of the new releases to customers not only could increase sales through the infrequent customers but also through the loyal customers too. What is more, customer loyalty generally would be increased and that is good news for that business and bad news for all the competitors who would just love to get their hands on some of the existing business.

Eventually you can go further than just trying to increase business from an old customer by selling them more of what they have bought already. As you develop the techniques and the ability to use your database more effectively, you can pinpoint areas of interest and target them even more directly. For example, you may not have to mail all your customers at any one time.

Taking the example of a video shop again, you could start to build up a profile of your customers' preferences by logging film types rented. Then, if you have a new blockbuster of a horror film released, you can mail all those customers who have rented a horror film from you to generate extra revenue. Or, if you are fairly confident that the new film will be rented out for some weeks to come, you could run a special offer on a group of films that are not being rented so much, aimed at the particular customer groups that have shown an interest in them previously.

**Direct mail allows you to be precise about who you wish to talk to if you have built up the correct information along the way.**

*Action Point*

Think about how you can build a profile of your customers. What makes them different? Do some customers buy only a small part of your range and would they buy other products from you if they were better informed ?

## CHAPTER 2
# Targeting your customers

Once you have decided that direct mail could form an effective part of your marketing campaign, how do you go about creating a mailshot that will work to bring you new business and to generate more business from your existing customers?

**There are two important elements of any direct mail campaign.** The first is the package that you send and the second is the list of people that you send the package to. Direct mail experts are agreed that it is far better to send a poor creative package to a well targeted list than it is to send a great package to a poorly targeted list. In short, the list of prospects is all-important and however superb your offer and however good your product or service may be, unless you are sending the details to contacts who are likely to be interested in the offer, then you'll be wasting your money.

Existing customers can be easy to target, especially if you already have them on a list somewhere. However, new prospects may be more difficult to get hold of. Apart from your existing customers, most businesses will have a list of general enquiries - people who enquired about a product from you sometime in the past but have not yet bought. In a later chapter I will be emphasising the need to both collect and keep this information, just as you should be keeping your existing customers on file. This group of *"enquirers"* may not have bought from you for a number of reasons including not being ready at the time or, unfortunately, making a decision to buy from someone else.

Not being ready to buy is a common reason for enquiries not to turn into sales immediately, especially if the products are high value items. Many customers will shop around and educate themselves when buying a more expensive item such as a stereo system, a television, a suite of furniture or a video unit. If you have a direct mail programme in place you may be able to turn more of these enquiries into sales by giving them the extra reason to buy from you - *the trigger we talked about earlier.*

You may have, therefore, both existing customers and *"enquirers"* to work with already and you can certainly tailor a mailer for both these groups. Note though that the mailer may not be the same for the two groups. If you really want your mailshot to be that much more effective you probably need a slightly different message for each.

For example, if you are selling high value items, you may want to build loyalty with your existing customers by offering them a special deal on a particular new range of products, while you may wish to generate the first sale from those people who have enquired about the products by offering them a special discount off the full range to tempt them a little more. Unless you know exactly what the customer has bought and what they may be interested in, it is harder to target specific offers. Once again, the value of taking and recording exact details of your customers purchases and enquiries is highlighted.

*Action Point*
Do you have a database policy ? If not spend some time thinking about what equipment you might need and make plans to be a leader in this field.

## TALKING TO PEOPLE YOU DON'T YET KNOW ...

To expand your customer base through the direct mail route you may wish to look at other options to build your list of targets. These days you can get hold of almost any contact list you wish, within reason. If you are looking for a list of businesses that have between 25 and 50 employees, do not own a forklift truck and are situated on industrial sites that are 10 years old or less, you can most probably get one. Lists like these can be rented from specialist companies which you may be able to find in Yellow Pages under *"Direct Mail"*. Rentals of lists works very simply. All you do is to choose the list you would like, decide how many you would like to have (there may be a minimum quantity involved) and decide whether you would like to have them on labels or disk to run off on your own computer.

**You only rent the list though, you do not buy it.** This means that you only get to use the list once and you cannot keep it on your own computer system to use again. Neither can you photocopy the labels to use a second time. Within every list you rent are dummy names. These are names and addresses that may be members of staff or someone else who is connected to the company you are renting the list from. This way, the renting company gets to view the material you actually send to the list - just in case it is different from the material you have told them that you are sending.

The dummy names also receive the second mailer if you use the list twice, and guess what? That's right, first you get billed again and then you probably either get your knuckles badly rapped or even get sued and can never use the company again, so it really isn't very clever to misuse the list or abuse the trust of the list company.

This type of list building exercise can be very cost effective, is really simple and, if you can get hold of a really well targeted list, can provide you with additional business fairly simply. Of course, if a contact from the rented list does respond to your mailing, then they are yours to keep forever.

If you don't feel that you are ready to go the whole way and use a rented list, or your customer type is such that finding a list would be difficult, then how do you go about finding new contacts to mail to?

## OTHER WAYS OF FINDING MORE OF THE SAME ...

*We're back to targeting again.* In the section on advertising I suggested that a good way of deciding where to advertise would be to follow companies who may be selling to a similar customer group. In the same way you find new customers by renting names from a non-competing company selling to a similar profile of customer and willing to release their names and addresses.

For example, if you are selling home improvement products, you could assume that customers of a conservatory company may be interested in some of your items. Customers who have bought conservatories are obviously interested in improving their home and that's who you are looking for. So, by building up a picture of what type of customer you should target and their interests, you can match other customer groups who might be worth considering.

Don't get me wrong, building a potential customer base this way isn't all sweetness and light. For one thing, you may have a considerable job to persuade companies to rent you their lists. In a number of cases you'll be surprised to learn that the companies you contact are doing nothing with their lists themselves and that they have never considered renting out their list to anyone else. Don't let this put you off, go in with the attitude that there has to be a first time and, more especially, that you don't get anything without asking for it.

The worse that can happen is that they say no. Then you are no worse off than before. Spending time trying to set a deal like this up is, I believe, time very well spent, simply because if you do get a deal and you put together an effective mailer, then the rewards could be far greater and much more cost effective than spending your budget week after week in the local or national press on advertising.

*Like everything in life, of course, there are compromises.*

If the company you have contacted refuses to release the list, and your product or service is non-competing, then why not ask them if they would consider an insert in their next mailing to their customers for which you will pay a percentage of the cost. Some companies will like this idea. However, you have to bear in mind also that some companies won't wish to have your leaflet in with their details as it may complicate their message or even overpower their own details. This is something you should think carefully about if the boot is ever on the other foot and you are approached to send other details out with your own.

Another variation on the same theme would be to request that your details are inserted along with their information into the packages they send their new enquiries. You could even offer to insert their details into your mailings to enquirers. Obviously, this works best if the two companies are generating a similar amount of enquiries.

Clearly then, by analysing what type of customer you already have, you can find others with the same profile and build both your customer base and your sales consistently. The same principles apply if you are a business-to-business company.

---

*Action Point*

Which other products would your customers tend to buy? Is there a trend? Which companies either locally, regionally or nationally sell these other products? Are they willing to rent a customer list to you?

*C H A P T E R  3*

# Making your mailer as powerful as possible

When you know who you are going to mail it's time to make decisions about the package that you are going to send. In its simplest form, a direct mail package will consist of:

- An Envelope

- A Letter

- A Brochure

*A DIRECT MAIL PACKAGE*

There are a number of other elements that you can include, but for now let's just take a look at these three.

The envelope may seem to a very mundane element to highlight as being rather important; surely an envelope is just an envelope isn't it?

*Not really no, at least not in the direct mail world.* You could make a number of decisions about your envelope that will certainly make a difference to the success of your mailer. The first thing to decide about the envelope is the size that you will use.

How many times have you opened some information to find that inside the small thin envelope *(DL size)* there's a letter and colour brochure that has been stuffed into it and folded twice to make it fit? I know that every time it happens to me I feel that whoever sent me the information didn't really care what condition it arrives in and is therefore not that interested in having my business.

Just think of it, you spend a considerable amount designing and printing your A4 brochure, only to find that each time a potential customer is requesting information, someone in the office is almost rolling it up to make it fit the smallest envelope they can find! Let's face it, the difference in cost between the different sized envelopes can never be so great as to justify the defacing of one of the most important pieces of selling ammunition you have. Make sure that the envelope is big enough to take comfortably all the information you intend to send, without the material being folded at all.

Once you have decided on the size of envelope you are going to use, the next stage is to decide on the colour. *Yes, the colour!*

### White or manila or even a light blue with yellow dots?

There will be a larger difference in price here, but, if you can afford it, try to use white whenever you can unless you really want to make an impression and go for a coloured envelope. White looks nicer and gives the package a more upmarket feel. A coloured envelope will certainly get you noticed, but it may be wasted if the post is opened by anyone other than the target whom the mailer is aimed at. For example, many companies have their post opened by the receptionist or in a post room, so your more expensive envelope may go straight into the bin along with the rest, without making the desired impact on the target of the mailing.

Size and colour decided, the next question is whether or not to print on the envelope. If you are starting out down the direct mail route you may not want to go to the expense of printing on the envelope. However, printing can do a number of things for you. Your envelope gives you the opportunity to raise awareness of your company name. If you are selling to businesses, you may want a number of people in each company to recognise your name and your logo. Printing the company name on the envelope can be effective in this regard. One of the best positions you can choose for the name is on the flap where the envelope will be opened. That way you can be almost sure that it'll be seen.

**The real opportunity however is to print a message on the envelope that will help it to get opened with some interest.** This may be more appropriate if you are targeting private individuals or smaller businesses where there is more likelihood that the mailer will get opened by the person it is addressed to.

Take a look at the envelopes you are receiving either at home or into your business right now. Each day you'll get samples through the door that you can analyse, determine the effectiveness of and, if you like the idea - copy. Remember, as I have said before, there are very few really new ideas and so don't worry about pinching one you like and adapting it for your own use. The fact is that the idea was probably copied by the company you are copying off anyway and, what's more, your idea will get copied at some stage too if it's good enough.

The types of phases that are likely to help the envelope get opened will promise something to the reader. For example:

"Inside you'll find the answer to your dreams"

"Open now to take advantage of the best offer you'll get this year"

Or you could try the approach that aims to scare the reader into opening the envelope …

"Unless you want to be paying too much for your insurance, we think you should take a look inside"

**And then there's the style that almost challenges the reader …**

"Don't open this unless you want to become richer in seven days"

You can also use key words on the envelope to gain attention. Some examples might be…

SAVE … PRIVATE … SPECIAL … EXCLUSIVE … GUARANTEE ….

URGENT … CONFIDENTIAL …

These are called **trigger words** and they'll work well to gain the attention and to keep it long enough to get the envelope opened.

Finally, on the envelope, you will have to decide how to complete the address. There are a number of choices here too. The most basic method of addressing is the handwritten address. This, of course, is the most laborious and probably the only option if you haven't got a computer to run a mailing list from. Although the handwritten addresses are a real pain if you are completing a large number, it is actually the most effective style. This is because it looks so much more personal than the computer typeface, and it is of course, because it has taken far longer. In fact, large companies using sophisticated direct marketing techniques sometimes use the handwritten style themselves to try to increase the effectiveness of the mailer.

If you are going to send handwritten envelopes, you may like to consider making a master copy and photocopying onto *"Butterfly Labels"* which are available through most stationery suppliers. This way, at least you'll be writing the labels out just the once and you'll be able to use them again and again. This is important because it is recognised that direct mail is far more effective after a number of mailings (six or seven) to an address or contact - *yes, it can be a long haul, but the rewards are there if you stick with it.*

## WHAT'S IN A NAME ...

What happens if you don't know the name of the contact that you are targeting? Well, it is far better to address a mailing to *"The Managing Director"* than to send it into a company with no direction and hope that your package gets to the right person. If the person who opens the mail is not the target for the information they are not usually going to spend a deal of time pawing their way through the contents of your envelope to try to work out who to pass it to.

The worst possible result would be if they directed it wrongly to someone not interested in your product and for whom it holds absolutely no relevance. People get too much mail these days to spend time on things that they cannot instantly recognise as a priority and so your mailer will immediately be destined for the bin. If your mailer is targeted to the person who buys the print for a company and you do not have a name, then *"To the Print Buyer"* is more likely to succeed. At least it gives the receptionist or post room team a clue where to direct the information.

The next stage is to ensure that, once the envelope is opened, your information or offer has the best possible chance of being read by the right person and acted upon. A strong letter will help to get the message across.

## MAKING THE MOST OF YOUR LETTER ...

There are a number of jobs that you may wish your letter to do for you. They can include:

- Informing your contact of a change or development of a product or service.

- Encouraging your contact to send off for further information.

- Persuading your contact to make a decision to spend money on a product and send back a completed order form.

Whatever you are trying to achieve with your letter you will find that it will be far more effective if you follow a few simple guidelines which we will discuss shortly.

First of all though - *Why do you need to send a letter in the first place if you are enclosing a product brochure as well?*

The morning I was writing this section of the book I opened two mailers at my home. I had requested information from both the companies concerned. The first envelope contained a photocopied sheet and a compliments slip which advised me that the leaflet was out of print for the moment. The second envelope contained all the correct elements of an effective direct mail package. Inside the second envelope (which was printed with details of the company name and the offer they were promoting) was a four page letter, a booklet explaining the product, a small leaflet which gave details of the guarantee, an order form and an envelope to use in which to send back my order.

**I wrote out a cheque for the second product and placed the information on the first product in the bin!** Not surprising really.

It is easy to see which mailer was the most effective. Of course, the second mailer took a great deal more effort to put together and will have cost more. However, really the surprising thing was that the package produced properly and professionally was promoting an item costing £39.95 while the photocopied sheet was trying to sell a product with a retail value of £121.00!

The simple fact of the matter is that one package was working for the company and the second package probably wasn't. Even if the second rate package was producing results, it certainly wouldn't be nearly as effective as it could have been with the correct treatment.

You have a clear and easy choice. Either spend time and with a little thought create an effective mailer which will produce you results, or take the easy way out and send a second class mailer that will, more often than not, end up in the bin.

The letter is a very important element in your mailer. Whatever you are sending to a potential customer, never, never let it go out without some kind of letter, even if it is a three lined *"thank you for sending for the information"* note. Sometimes a compliments slip is attached to a brochure - with nothing written on it. Surely this has to be a waste of time and of stationery. It certainly isn't saying too much to the customer. Spend a little more time and produce a few lines which may make all the difference.

The first rule to remember when writing a letter in a direct mail package is this -

**If you are sending a package that is asking the customer to send off for further information, keep the letter short.**

The reason is that you don't want to include all the product details since the customer may feel that all the information they need to make a decision on whether or not to purchase is in the pack. Then they may not contact you again. The letter accompanying a package aimed at creating a further response should give few details of the product and should attempt to create further questions in the mind of the recipient so that they will want to know more.

The second rule is -

**When you are writing a letter that is aiming to sell a product directly off the page, longer copy is better.**

If you want the customer to take out their cheque book *(just as I did this morning)* and to pay for a product they may never have seen before, then, generally, the longer the letter the better. If you remember I said the package that made me take action had a four page letter included among other things. The letter covered all the reasons why I should write out the cheque and answered most of the questions which may have prevented me from doing so. You'll need a reasonably long letter to convince the reader to part with their money and as you will have only one chance to do so, you may as well make it your best effort and give them every conceivable reason to make that positive decision.

Clearly, unless you are very gifted, these tips aren't going to enable you to produce an award winning direct mail letter the first time you sit down and put pen to paper. Writing effective direct mail copy is an art and something that the best copywriters get paid a great deal of money to produce. However, you will be able to make your letters more effective and you will be able to improve them gradually simply by following some of these pointers.

**One of the simplest and easiest ways to get better at this particular job is to collect as many good examples of effective direct mail letter writing and to learn from them.** Whatever comes through your door or passes over your desk, view with a new critical eye and if you see a phase or sentence you like or you are impressed with the layout of a particular letter, save it in your snatch file for the future.

As I have mentioned, professional direct mail copywriting is indeed an art and it may

*Quick Tip*

If you aren't sure what you should be saying in a covering letter, send for details from your competitors. If they have a strong covering letter you're sure to get a few ideas and have an opportunity to make your pack more effective.

well be that, in the course of your development you may want to use a professional to increase the effectiveness of your promotional material or maybe to produce a new creative idea for you. Once again, make the most of what's about. If you pick up some material you like, think about contacting the company and ask who produced it. At least then when you're ready for help you will know where to contact someone who has produced what you consider to be good work. But that's for the future. Here's some useful tips to use when putting a letter together for the first time.

## THE MECHANICS OF THE LETTER ...

I promised right at the start of this book that it wouldn't be full of theory - just practical ideas that you could use right away and I hope that so far you have found that to be the case. However, there is one piece of theory that I feel should be included and it's something that I have found to be very useful over the years.

The theory is the **A.I.D.A.** approach to writing direct mail letters. It is very simple to use. A.I.D.A. stands for the following:

**A  Attention**

**I  Interest**

**D  Desire**

**A  Action**

A.I.D.A. is a framework to help you build your letter and if you develop your work around these four elements, you should end up with a powerful and effective communication every time. *So, how does it work?*

**A is for attention.** You only have a certain amount of time (usually a very small amount) to grab the attention of the reader when the letter is taken out of the envelope. Just note how long it takes you to decide that the information you have picked up isn't of any interest to you the next time you put a mailer in the bin ! You must use this very limited time in the best way that you can and that means strongly highlighting your most important benefit very early into your letter.

How many times have you received a letter from a business trying to sell you something only to find that the first two paragraphs are all about the company, when it was formed, who owns it and what's on the menu in the works canteen every Thursday! This type of letter isn't going to get your attention simply because it isn't really selling you anything at all. You must hit the reader with a benefit which he can relate to before he has time to switch off and discard your mailing package.

For example, if you were selling a new imaginary filing system, there are two ways of producing the beginning of a letter aimed at persuading your target to buy.

## METHOD NO. 1

Dear Sir,

I am writing to you to give you details of a new product recently introduced by Filex, the leading distributor of filing systems in the UK since 1956.

Made to extremely high standards in our 13,000 sq. ft factory in South Wales and distributed through our subsidiary company Distrofile, our new product has been manufactured for six months and is now available in your area.

## METHOD NO. 2

Dear Customer,

Struggling for office space ? The new Filex filing system is the answer to your paperwork problems. That's right, if you are spending more time looking for your papers than actually working on them right now, the unique Filex can help you save hours and keep your files looking neat and tidy.

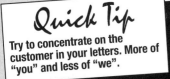

**Quick Tip**

Try to concentrate on the customer in your letters. More of "you" and less of "we".

I hope that the difference between the two styles is clear to see. In the first example, the letter isn't selling the benefits of owning a Filex system, it is only giving information about the company. How often do you buy a product because of the size of the warehouse or the location of the business? *In fact, in this example there is no clear benefit linked to the information given.*

The second example actually highlights the benefit of owning a Filex system. You can be sure that if you are having real difficulties with your paperwork and this letter lands on your desk, then you are going to look twice at it and, with any luck, continue to read it. **That is the critical stage** - getting your potential customer to read on past the first few lines.

So, the first point to remember is always to highlight your most important benefit first. In the case of Filex it is the ability to save time due to the organisational qualities of the product, not how it is made, what it looks like or in which colours it can be supplied - all that will come later. Remember, the customer will be buying a system which helps them to manage their paperwork - not metal or cardboard components.

Notice also that the first letter was started with a very formal *"dear sir"* while the second example used *"dear customer"*. Try to make the beginning of your letter as friendly and as targeted as possible. If you are mailing to people interested in gardening then *"dear gardening enthusiast"* is a good start. Use *"dear friend"* if you can't think of anything else.

**There's another way to make the start of your letter more powerful too.** When we are advertising we are very keen to get the headline correct. In the same way your letter can use a headline too, at the top of the page, spelling out exactly why the reader should pick up the letter and find out what it has to say.

So the start of the Filex letter could become:

### FILES IN A REAL MESS ? HERE'S YOUR ANSWER

**A was for attention. I is for interest.**

The next stage after gaining the attention of the reader is to create the interest in the product. We can then expand on the benefits we have already highlighted. The letter may continue:

" We all know how frustrating it is when you can't lay your hands on that vital piece of paper at the right moment and these days, with more and more information being passed between us, it can be a real problem to keep on top of. Not with Filex helping out. Filex is a new concept in filing that will help sort out your files in an easy to understand way and ensure that when you want something quickly you can put your finger on it every time within seconds!"

Once the interest is built into the letter, the potential customer is starting to think that they might wish to own this product and now is the right time to start the third stage of the letter - to create the desire to buy or to take action.

**A is for attention, I is for interest, D is for desire.**

We may continue like this:

"With a Filex system in your office you'll be the envy of all your colleagues, because not only will you have a super efficient system, but you'll also have the opportunity to have the tidiest office around too. And that's not all. The Filex system looks great. Made from best quality mahogany it will enhance any office. You can choose from a selection of beautiful colours to match your existing furniture."

Finally, when you have built up your letter using the first three stages (and bear in mind that I am just trying to show examples and not trying to write a complete letter with this exercise), you will end the letter with the action element.

**A is for attention, I is for interest, D is for desire and A is for action.**

Collect a number of direct mail letters over the next few weeks. Unless you live somewhere very out of the way you are going to receive a number either into your business or at home. Study them to see if there is a letter amongst them that gives you plenty of information but doesn't let you know what to do next. Not telling the reader what to do next is one of the main reasons the effectiveness of any letter is weakened. If the examples you collect are from large companies, the chances are that each and every one of them will be crammed full of *"calls to action"* all the way through.

Don't be shy about asking the customer to take action. After all, you have spend time and money trying to persuade them to take an interest in your product. At least make it easy for them to buy if they want to.

Our imaginary letter might end like this:

"So, how can you get to see a Filex system for yourself? Well, you won't find it in any shops, but we will send you a sample section free of charge to try. All you have to do to get your own free sample is to fill in the pre-paid card and return it today. If you really can't wait to get hold of your free sample of this amazing new system that could do so much for you, telephone us on *** **** *** and speak to Jackie. She'll be happy to arrange for your free sample to be sent to you straight away. Remember, the Filex system isn't available anywhere else so don't miss out. Post your request card now."

In this example I have asked the customer to send off for further information and a free sample. If you were aiming to get the customer to send off money for the system without further information, then you would need to write a much longer letter with more details such as exactly how the system works and giving many more benefits and reasons to purchase. In a longer letter you need to be using many more features and benefits. Even the smallest feature or benefit becomes very important to help the reader make the buying decision and to part with their cash.

## INCREASING RESPONSE FURTHER ...

After you have used the A.I.D.A. system to build the framework of your letter, there are a number of other ideas that will make your promotion even more effective.

**The first point is never to assume that the reader knows anything about the product or service that you are offering.** This is sometimes very difficult to remember as we all tend to be very closely involved with our particular products and forget that the terms we use or the points we make may not be fully understood as easily by someone reading about it for the very first time.

Ask yourself whether the points you are trying to put across really are easy to understand and, better still, test your words out on someone who doesn't have anything to do with your business such as a friend or relative. They will be able to highlight any points that sound complicated or too technical and you'll have the opportunity to put it right before being distributed to hundreds or maybe thousands of potential customers who may stop reading because they cannot understand what you are trying to tell them.

Beware of too many jargon words that you know the meaning of but that the readers may not. They won't take the time out to ask you what you mean - *they just won't get back to you.* It is important to always remember that customers don't like to feel stupid, so never assume that they will understand.

## MORE TRICKS OF THE TRADE ...

As I have mentioned, the art of writing good direct mail copy is very involved. However, there are a number of simple rules to remember that will make your letters easier to read and which will ensure that you get your message across in a clear and concise way.

One of the first rules to remember is to indent your paragraphs just like I have done in this book. It makes the letter look as though it will be easier to read. Also, don't set the page so that the lines are exactly the same length (this is known as justifying your lines). Not being *"justified"* makes it easier to read. There is something daunting about a page of words that are justified and with the paragraphs starting at the edge of the page.

And, on the subject of paragraphs, don't make them too long. A large number of short paragraphs has got to be better than just one or two that go on and on for ever. **Small bites of information have a better chance of being digested than large helpings.**

The same goes for sentences too; keep them as short as possible and use words that you think that your customer would use. Try to get into the mind of your customer and write as if you were talking to them face to face. Keep the majority of your words short and try not to use longer words just for effect because the chances are that it will be detrimental and it will result in readers switching off because of it. **Don't try to be too clever.**

It doesn't happen so much these days, but letters that start *"I write in reply to your communication dated 25th"* certainly aren't using the snappy language you would use if you were face to face with the customer. Don't get too hung up on grammar. If you break the rules but it sounds good and is easy to read, then break the rules.

In the direct mail letters you have received recently you may notice that some words or sentences are underlined. You can even underline a whole paragraph if you want to really emphasise a point. Many readers will browse through the letter first time around, picking out any points that are of interest to them. This is partly due to the fact that more of us are becoming conditioned to pulling the basics from a direct mail communication in just the way the writers have intended. Therefore try to ensure that your most important points are always jumping off the page.

Another simple trick is to mark the side of the page with a line or two, again to highlight an important point that you really want to be noticed. The lines can either be straight or freehand, it doesn't matter which. Following on from this you can even write notes in the margin to strengthen a point you are making - notes like this are almost certain to get read, even before the rest of the letter in most cases. But, if you are going to make notes in the margins, then choose the left hand side margin as it is thought to be more effective.

If you think that you may like to use margin notes you can design your letter so that you have wider margins to work with, making sure that your notes don't look too cramped. *Read this now.*

Carefully consider the typeface you are going to use. Professional copywriters will think long and hard about typefaces. A different typeface can help to pull out a particular point and help to break up the letter. **Bold also works to highlight words, a sentence or even a paragraph.** Beware of using too many typefaces in one letter though as this can sometimes look a little confusing and messy.

Take some time to think about the size of the typeface you need to use. Remember if you are dealing with older customers that they might have some trouble reading very small print and so you should take the typeface up in size whenever possible. Fancy styles may also be harder to read for older customers who may see them as being a little too "flashy".

One of the most effective typefaces to use is the standard typewriter typeface. Even if you are producing thousands of letters, by using the typewriter typeface you are giving the impression of a more personal letter as most people associate a typewriter with a *"one off"* communication.

**Now here's a really simple rule which works so well but is so easy to implement.** Always try to break a page in the middle of a sentence. This way the reader will be more likely to turn the page to continue reading. If you end the page at the end of a sentence, then you are providing the reader with a natural break and an excuse to stop reading altogether.

One thing on a letter is nearly always read and sometimes read before anything else. **It is the P.S.** Try to incorporate a P.S. into every letter you write and use the P.S. to reinforce a message or offer that you may have already mentioned in the letter. Going back to the letter for the Filex system for example, the P.S. could read:

**P.S. - Don't forget that the amazing Filex system can help you to save time as well as organising your paperwork!**

In this example we are highlighting a benefit that appeared at the beginning of the letter. Using the P.S. in this way may mean that the potential customer becomes interested in the product due to the P.S. and then reads the letter more fully.

Another use of the P.S. could have been:

**P.S. - Don't miss out on this great opportunity, send for your free sample today!**

Here we are reinforcing the action that we want the reader to take.

Another very useful component of a direct mail letter is what is known as a Johnson Box.

You might use a Johnson Box for some technical information or for a customer testimonial. It works for most things when you want to spotlight a specific point.

> A Johnson Box is simply a box in the body of the letter that highlights specific information just like this.

## GETTING YOUR CUSTOMERS TO DO THE SELLING ...

Customer testimonials are very powerful and if you can use them do so. Just a word of warning though. Don't continue to use them for years on end unless you check that the customer still thinks that you are the bee's knees. If you are using customer testimonials, try to link them to the benefits you are highlighting in the letter.

**The best way to produce a customer testimonial is to write it yourself and then get them to agree it!** This isn't so underhand as it sounds since whilst many customers would be willing to give a testimonial they don't really know what to say. Whether you are going to see them face to face or interview them on the telephone, just make some notes about what they are telling you and then fashion them into an easy-to-read and powerful few lines. Then call them back to run through the words with them and get their approval.

It's best to get the approval in writing, especially if the testimonial forms a large part of the campaign or it is going to be very high profile. Always give your contact an idea of where their testimonial is likely to appear (i.e. literature, letter or poster). That way they'll

*Quick Tip*

If you are mailing a reasonable quantity, consider printing the material instead of photo-copying. Unless you have a very good copier the quality just won't be as good as it should be. At the end of the day you may well find that printing is actually cheaper anyway, especially if you are intending to use the material time after time.

be no nasty shocks when they pick up the Radio Times and see their name and words staring back at them. A picture will add credibility alongside the words.

Another tip to make your letter more effective and more believable is to be as specific as you can when making claims or giving details of product performance. Saying that the new product will increase productivity by over 4.0% is far more effective than saying that it will increase productivity considerably. Saying that it will increase productivity by an even more specific 4.2% is even more powerful. Developing this even further, a claim that the product will increase productivity 4.2% in just 14 days is even better. But make sure that you can back up your claims with facts, or the Advertising Standards might make life difficult for you - and rightly so.

To recap, remember to bear in mind the following points when you are looking to prepare a powerful direct mail letter.

## CHECKLIST 5 – CREATING A DIRECT MAIL LETTER

1. Decide how long your letter needs to be. Is it a shorter letter to get the customer interested in sending off for further details or is it a longer letter giving the customer all the reasons why they should buy the product?

2. Have you created a strong headline for your letter?

3. What are you going to call your potential customer, "Dear Friend", "Dear Colleague" etc.

4. Remember the A.I.D.A. framework to pull your reader through the letter.

5. Are you able to break the pages in the middle of a sentence to make sure the reader doesn't turn off?

6. Don't forget a P.S.

7. Can you highlight certain words, phrases, sentences or full paragraphs to make the letter more effective?

8. Is there room or need for a Johnson Box?

9. Can you use margin lines or notes to strengthen points?

10. Are there any customer testimonials that you can use?

11. Put the letter aside for a little time before you make your final decision.

Remember that a good direct mail letter shouldn't only be used when you are considering a mailing programme to a specific list of new or existing contacts. You should be including a powerful letter with everything you are sending out to customers.

## ALSO IN THE PACK ...

Along with your letter you will almost certainly want to send other information too. However, what you send will depend on what you are trying to achieve with the mailing package. If you are looking to generate sales, then you will want to send a product brochure along with an order form too, whereas if you have designed your mailshot to generate further response, product details might not be included at this stage, or, if they are, they may be much less detailed.

**Sometimes a second letter is included in the package.** You may have seen this in any examples you have received yourself. This second letter is generally a different size to the original letter and probably signed by someone else. It may also be produced on a different coloured paper and use different typestyles to the original. This is called a *"lift letter"* and is used to strengthen the arguments put forward in the first letter. You will see them with headlines such as:

**"Don't read this unless you are convinced that our offer is genuine"**

In short it is aimed at catching the doubters and turning them around. It might even be written in a testimonial style from an existing customer.

If you use a response card or order form as part of the pack, try to ensure that they are really easy to complete. The order form and response card tend to get forgotten when the creative minds are at work, but they are two of the most important elements in the pack. After all, if they don't work then neither does the mailer.

Both order forms and response cards can be "beefed up" and have strong "calls to action" on them by using phrases such as *"post today" or "don't delay, send your order now"*. Providing an envelope for the response will also increase the numbers received as will using a freepost address. Anything you can do to make it easier for the customer to respond will reap benefits.

Somewhere in your pack, and certainly within your main letter, you will want to include an offer of some kind. Offers increase response, whether it is a percentage discount if sent within seven days or a free gift of some sort when they buy. Deadlines are important too, making sure that the customer is pushed into action sooner rather than later. A **free 30 day trial** may also increase response. Customers don't seem to think of a free trial as a purchase so much, although quite clearly it is the same thing in the end.

*Be careful with the free gifts though.* It is important to strike the right balance between what is strong enough to get the initial response and too expensive to supply in large numbers. You will have to accept that the number of replies you receive with a free gift offer will be artificially high and that some of those responding will be doing so just for the gift. It is important to think about the gift carefully and to try to offer something which is in some way related to the product that you are selling or the market you are trying to attract. This way, anyone responding to the free gift should also be at least interested in the product you are selling.

Be careful with discounts too. Don't try to make the product look too cheap as it will turn some potential customers off.

One way to increase the chances of getting your envelope opened is to send a free sample with the mailer in the first place. You will have probably received a mailer with a free pen enclosed, or a keyring. Anything that will make the envelope feel interesting. Let's face it, when you receive a package with something enclosed that you can feel but cannot see, it is very difficult not to open it to see what's inside. Sending an object relating to your product, or even a piece of the product itself can be an effective tool to use in certain circumstances.

## TO SUM UP ...

There are a number of ways in which direct mail can be an effective tool for your business. Existing customers or new, potential customers - *direct mail can be used to increase sales from all types of contacts.* Direct mail packs can be very sophisticated, but you don't have to include all the elements to start with. Just the fact that you are talking to both new and existing contacts will mean that you will have the opportunity to increase your business.

One of the most important tasks for any business must surely be to get their customer details into a form where they can start to use them to keep in touch on a regular basis. Whether you intend to send out mailings once a year or once a week, getting the foundations of a programme built is of the utmost importance. Maybe you don't feel as though you want to go to the expense of computerisation right now. That's fine, but you can still organise a manual database which will take you further forward and will give you that vital edge over your competition.

**Direct mail isn't just about selling more products,** although obviously it's an important element. Direct mail is also very much about building a lasting relationship with your customers, keeping them informed and protecting them from other companies which may come along and try to take them from under your nose. Having said that, it does afford you the opportunity to introduce new products to customers who may not have had the chance to see them before.

You will probably have a number of different categories of names and addresses somewhere within your business right now. Apart from existing customers, there may also be a number of general enquirers who haven't yet bought from you. These two categories, along with other types of leads which you may have, can be used straight away with a direct mail programme. The messages that you will want to get across to your existing customers may well be different than the messages you will want to deliver to people who have not yet bought from you. Direct mail offers you this flexibility.

Once you have spent time putting together a direct mail package, you will want to keep it as your *"control"*. That is to say something against which you can measure the success of new ideas. There is little point in changing what you are sending if you have no idea whether the new pack is performing any better than the old pack which has produced results for you in the past. Some of the most productive direct mail packs haven't been changed much for years, simply because nothing else has proved to be more effective. The message is, if you have something that is working for you, make sure that any changes are for the better.

## BUILDING MORE OF THE SAME ...

You can build your mailing lists in a number of different ways. As previously mentioned, lists can be rented and the chances are that whatever business you are in you will be able to find a list which relates pretty closely to the type of customer you would like to talk to. However, there are other, less expensive, methods of building a list too. For example, if you receive trade magazines you will probably be able to find new contacts in them. One of the most useful sections is *"recruitment"*, where you may find pages and pages of names and addresses of prime contacts.

Directories, of course, as we have also discussed, can be very useful for list building. A trip to the local library can get the ball rolling, but each particular industry has its own goldmine of directories hidden away, just waiting to be found.

If you are intending to enter your contacts onto computer, you will want to make sure that you are registered under the Data Protection Act. The offices of the Data Protection Registrar provides guidance on the laws governing the holding and use of personal data and it is wise to contact them for one of their information packs. They are based in Wilmslow, Cheshire.

If you do build a database, especially if you have your records on computer and easily retrievable, you will have built something that will be of tremendous value to your company. You will also have something that may be of value to others too and it may well be that eventually you will be in a position to rent your list to non-competing organisations. You may be in a position to offer a list swop too, so that you are getting new potential customers as part of the deal.

Whilst this shouldn't be a major consideration right now, if you are intending to build a large database then it is something that you should be aware of for the future, as it could end up paying for the upkeep of your own list in years to come. In short, you could be sitting on a new profit centre.

**Direct mail has become one of the most valuable tools in the marketing armoury.** Quite clearly, the direct mail industry will continue to grow, safe in the knowledge that this method of promoting to customers is one of the most cost effective possible if you get it right. It can be quite simple to achieve results and it is a form of marketing that the vast majority of businesses will be able to adopt without too much trouble. With this in mind, my advice would be to consider it carefully and, if you aren't already using it, to try it out for yourself - *you may get to like it quite a lot !*

# Summary Points

1. Learn more about direct mail by studying the material you are being sent both at work and at home.

2. If you haven't already organised your customer contacts, consider the various options which will enable you to keep in touch.

3. Remember that the list of people that you send information to is more important than the content of your mailer. Targeting is the key.

4. Although the list is very important, don't underestimate the importance of making your mailing as powerful as possible. Make sure that the information your customers receive is going to impress them.

5. Follow the A.I.D.A. approach to letter writing.

6. Continually build your database by being on the lookout for new contacts. Consider purchasing contacts if you can find a suitable list.

*SECTION FOUR*

# How to make a proper exhibition of yourself

" *DON'T LOOK AT THEM – THEY'LL GO AWAY SOON* "

**NOTES**

*CHAPTER 1*
# Choosing the right exhibition

You'd be surprised how many companies attend exhibitions and don't give themselves even half a chance of getting anything out of them. They seem to think that once the stand space is booked there's nothing left to attend to, but there is. If you're going to get the most out of any exhibition, you have to plan carefully, put a little thought into your display and make sure that you go with the right frame of mind.

This section deals with all the points you will have to consider to ensure that you aren't wasting your money, from making sure that the exhibition is the right one for you to booking the right space, making your stand work and how to get the most from your staff during the event.

**Exhibitions are a different way of selling.** The customer comes to you and, as you are neither in their office nor your showroom, there is less pressure on both of you. However, having said that, you are not on your own. There are many other distractions going on and so the trick is to use whatever images and experiences you can to gain the attention of your potential market.

## MAKING SURE YOU ARE IN THE RIGHT PLACE ...

*But how do you know that the exhibition is right for you in the first place?* Well, it's back to targeting again as we discussed in the section on advertising. If you think that the exhibition is going to attract the type of customers you feel are going to be in the market for your products, that's a good start.

You will probably need more information about the exhibition before you commit yourself. There are a number of simple questions to ask exhibition organisers which may point you in the right direction. Some of them are:

- Has the exhibition been held before?

- What was the attendance the last time it was held? Was it up or down on the previous year?

- What level of attendance is being aimed at for this year's show?

- Do they have a breakdown of the customer type attending?

- How did they promote the show last time?

- What extra or different promotions are they running to help increase the attendance at this year's show?

- What type of company is attending, either by size or by product?

If you have a choice of a number of exhibitions to attend and you cannot afford to be at them all, you may wish to make your decision on the basis of how many visitors you will get to see per pound spent. If all the exhibitions are similar, then this is as good a way as any to make the choice.

Using the above checklist will give you some indication of whether the exhibition is likely to attract the type of customer you are looking for. For example, if the organisers tell you that their major promotional campaign for the show is running in a trade magazine which just isn't the type of material that your customers would read, it may indicate that you won't want to be at the show unless there are other plans that will attract the people you are specifically aiming for.

Obviously, if the exhibition is running for the first year, then you will have a lot less information to base your decision on, but you should still be able to get a good idea of whether the organisers are tuned in to the market or whether, as can be the case, the organisers aren't doing the sort of groundwork necessary to fill the show with visitors. Getting visitors into any show takes a great deal of effort and if you feel that the effort isn't being made, you can be fairly sure that the exhibition will be less busy than you would like it to be.

If you are starting in business or you have decided to be more aggressive in your marketing and you are looking to increase sales by taking a part of your competitors' share, then take a look at where they are exhibiting and if they have attended the same exhibition for a few years, the chances are that it provides them with a level of potential customers that they are happy with.

## HAVING A REASON TO BE THERE ...

Before you make the final decision about whether or not to attend an exhibition, you should also have thought out the particular objectives that you would like to achieve by being there. If you cannot list any objectives, you may be wasting your money attending, so it is worthwhile taking the time to complete this task.

Unfortunately, many companies attending shows don't go with any specific aims which is very evident by their stand displays and the way that they approach the exhibition. Poor or unclear aims may be to *"fly the flag"* or *"because we are leaders in the Industry"*. The aims and objectives that you should be looking to establish and achieve each time you exhibit should be far more specific and measurable, such as:

- **Selling £5,000 worth of product X**

- **Signing up eight new distributors**

- **Taking orders for over £10,000 from existing customers**

- **Receiving publicity in four trade journals**

- **To be seen to be the most professional company in the industry**

- **To launch the new corporate identity**

All the above are measurable and can be monitored day by day at the show. Even if you have attended the same exhibition for five or six years you should be doing this exercise, since you may have fallen into the trap of just turning up at the exhibition and expecting it to happen for you.

*C H A P T E R   2*
# Making the right decisions about space

When you have decided whether or not to attend a particular exhibition, then you have another decision to make fairly quickly. That is to either book a preferred position or to wait and see if you can get a cheaper space later on.

*One important point.* Never, never, let the show organisers allocate you a space if you can choose one yourself. Your space position can be crucial and should not be made by anyone other than yourself.

There is always a temptation to find out where the loading bays are and to try to get as close to them as possible, just to make it easier to get your products in and out of the exhibition. Don't be tempted to base your selection on this criteria. If you do, you'll almost certainly be wasting an opportunity to get the most out of the exhibition, just for the sake of a few yards less to carry your equipment - what an unprofessional judgement to make !

**A good stand position in an exhibition can often make the difference between having a reasonable show and having a great show.** A good position is one where you are going to be highly visible to visitors who will have to pass your stand a number of times during the day. Generally, they are on the ends of aisles or near the entrances. A stand on the end of an aisle has three open sides and will attract traffic from up to six directions, whereas a stand on a terrace with only one open side will attract visitors from only two directions. An end site will be easier for the visitors to walk onto and will make them feel less trapped

*Action Point*

If you have found an exhibition that you would like to attend, but you can't afford the space costs, why not investigate whether there is another company in the same position with whom you could share the costs of a stand. As long as they are non-competing it may be a sensible option. The exhibition organisers may be able to point you in the right direction.

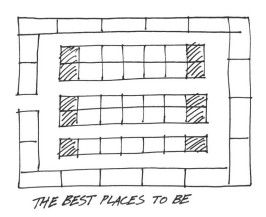

THE BEST PLACES TO BE

when they are on your stand. You will find that, generally, the end sites will be more expensive than the terrace sites, but the extra cost will almost certainly be worth it.

There are no hard and fast rules for booking stand space. Every venue is different. For example, sometimes the first stand inside an exhibition is just too close to the entrance. Visitors may miss the initial stands as they walk the first 20 yards into the show, sorting out their bags, reading the show catalogue or just generally getting themselves set for the day. So, if you are not sure, then book a stand, preferably with three open sides, in the main section of the exhibition and see how it goes.

There are ways to make more of the budget that you have allocated for the show. For example, if you can afford £500 for your stand space, you might find that it will buy you 12 square metres in the hall. You will find that there will be different shapes of stands which all amount to 12 square metres.

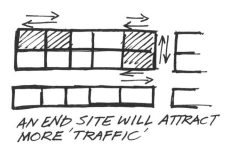

AN END SITE WILL ATTRACT MORE 'TRAFFIC'

For maximum impact, depending on the type of product you have on your stand, you should go for a space that will take a visitor the longest time to walk past. If, for example, you have booked a space that is 4m x 3m, you have just 4 metres of *"frontage"* for the visitor to walk past. If, however, you change the space to 6m x 2m, you have an extra 2 metres of "frontage" which could mean an extra couple of seconds exposure while the visitor is walking past your stand.

In a smaller show, although the principle is the same, it isn't quite as important as in the larger, busier show where every second counts if you are going to get that visitor onto your stand and interested in your products. A longer, thinner stand also helps you to display your products more effectively in some cases and creates that open feel to the stand which is important to encourage people onto your space.

As you can probably appreciate though, it can be a matter of compromise, since a long, thin space might be impossible at an end or corner site, so you will have to weigh up all the pros and cons and then make a judgement decision.

## GETTING EVEN MORE FOR YOUR MONEY ...

As you develop your exhibiting techniques, you will find that there are other ways to make the most of the space that you are buying. For example, two long stands opposite each other in an aisle may be more effective than one larger, squarer stand. This way you create the impression that the visitor is walking through your stand. If you then connect the spaces with signs either end and even put a muslin ceiling on the aisle you have effectively gained the aisle space as part of your stand.

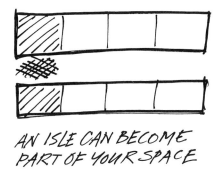

AN ISLE CAN BECOME
PART OF YOUR SPACE

Another method of creating higher exposure in a larger exhibition, and one that could be particularly effective if you have a number of separate products, is to take a number of smaller spaces throughout the exhibition. The benefits of this approach are to focus on the specific products for each stand and to increase the number of people that you will deal with. However, you do lose the *"corporate"* approach and if you are looking to create the big image then this method isn't for you.

Most exhibition halls have toilets and some have refreshment areas that are open during the show. These areas obviously attract a great many people throughout the day, so should your stand be near them? Well, it is a matter of personal choice. I myself have never really liked to be located near these areas because, although you do get a high volume of visitors, you also get congestion and a degree of mess too.

If you need some room off your stand to demonstrate your products then these spaces may not be such a good idea, as you may find that your attempted demonstration is in competition with a large crowd of visitors with absolutely no interest in your products. If you do decide to be near the bar, then you should realise that you could get empty glasses left on or about your stand and you may have to deal with all the hassle that goes hand in hand with being close to bars that are sometimes open all day long.

However, if you have a product that is in some way related to bar items, food or drink, or maybe a fun type item that would be best suited in a more relaxed atmosphere, then the bar area might be an effective one for you to go for.

On the subject of congestion, make sure that you are aware if there are narrower aisles in any part of the exhibition for any reason. **You don't want a stand with a small aisle alongside if at all possible.** Larger aisles make it easier for visitors to get around the exhibition. Sometimes visitors will even take a diversion around an area which looks more congested - not good news for the stands that are located in that area. Visitors also tend to move through tighter areas more quickly and take less notice of the stands in those areas, again because they feel and look too crowded.

## USING THE SPACE TO YOUR BEST ADVANTAGE ...

If there are any rest areas provided for visitors to relax during the day you may wish to be close to one of them. Again, you will want to make a decision based on the floor plans and to see just where the rest areas are located, but, if they still give you room to move around the outside of your stand comfortably and there looks like being little risk of congestion, they could increase the awareness of your stand in the show considerably.

**The reason is this.** Apart from attracting a large number of people who will be sitting and looking at your stand while resting, generally there will be no shell scheme used to construct the rest area. That is to say the area will not be built up with walls and fascias. If the area is in the body of the hall and if you take a space next door, visitors will be able to see your stand from much further away, looking through the rest area to spot you and giving you more time to impress them with your display.

And, don't forget, if you have a large number of people staring at your stand, you have a golden opportunity to be able to provide them with something to watch while they are waiting, so try to give them something of interest to look at such as a demonstration or display.

In the same way, if there are any exhibitors who take space only and do not then build themselves a high stand, using the floor space for smaller exhibits only, you will enjoy more exposure by booking a space opposite them so that visitors can once again see you from further away. Talk to the organisers and ask them if there are any companies who have stands like this in the show.

Making sure that exhibition visitors are aware of your stand for as long as possible before they actually reach it is something which will increase your profile in the show. You can achieved this cost effectively by securing a stand at the end of an isle. With any luck, visitors will have spotted your stand a number of times out the corner of their eye by the time that they reach you, especially if you have increased the height of your stand with a powerful sign placed above.

*The same principle applies to balcony sites.* If the exhibition is on two levels and there is a balcony which can be seen clearly from the ground floor, extra exposure can be achieved by booking one of the sites on the edge and draping a large sign over the balcony. You'll be using the back of your stand, a dead area, for some effect.

If, on the other hand, you prefer to be down below when there is a balcony used by visitors, then don't miss the opportunity to place a sign up high and, if possible, on the roof of your stand, so that you can communicate with the visitors even when they are some way from you.

Booking exhibition space is mostly all about compromises and you should be careful to make sure that if you are booking the type of spaces I have just mentioned, then you are doing so with your primary aims in mind and not just because it might get one over on the competition - *however satisfying that may be!!*

And what about the competition? Do you choose a stand near them or try to keep as well away as possible? Sometimes you won't have too much of a choice since some exhibitions are sectionalised. However, most shows aren't and you can locate wherever you want.

If you are a new company, then there are advantages to being close to your nearest competitors since if they are an established company, they will probably have been more active than yourselves in attracting both existing and new customers into the show. That has to be good news for you as their contacts will undoubtedly see your stand too. However, to be confident about placing your stand very close to your nearest competitor, you really have to be sure that what you are offering compares well and that your stand will look professional in comparison to their own. So the message really is that if you are confident that you have planned the show well and that your product and package are competitive, then one option must be to site yourself directly opposite and go for it!!

It isn't just your competitors you should be interested in when you are booking your own space though. Wherever you intend to have your stand, you should be finding out which companies are either side or opposite you. If you know of a very successful business attracting large numbers of visitors to their stand, you may wish to site yourself near them as you can then guarantee a busy area. However, be careful. *An overpowering company with an overpowering stand could make it very difficult for you to be heard and seen.*

On a practical note, it is also wise to find out which company is next to you at the show, especially if the stands are connected in any way. This avoids the problem of getting to the show only to find that one of the side walls of an adjoining company has been built up higher than normal for their own purposes, which closes off your own stand somewhat. At least if you know what to expect when you get into the hall you can plan ahead to use your space more effectively.

Just one more point about booking space at the show. It is wise to take into account how many staff you will have available on the stand. Putting too many salespeople onto a small stand is just as bad as putting too few onto a large stand. In the first instance you will end up with your salespeople fighting over visitors (especially if commission is involved) or half your staff wandering around the show because they can't get on their own stand, whilst in the second example you will create pressure on the staff to cover the area effectively. Either way you will end up with a stand that is a good deal less effective than it could be and one that visitors may feel is less than welcoming.

*CHAPTER 3*

# Designing a winning stand

After you have booked your stand and are happy about your position, you will then have to decide just what you are going to do with your space. Some exhibitions will provide you with a **shell scheme** whilst others will provide you with space only. A shell scheme is a basic unit which is generally comprised of walls, a fascia board and sometimes electrics and lighting. Space only is exactly that. You walk into the hall and you have a concrete floor to work with. Space only is generally chosen if you are intending to design and build a stand yourself or you intend to use a mobile exhibition system.

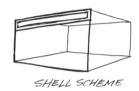

SHELL SCHEME

If you decide to take the shell scheme for your stand it means that you will be able to walk into the hall and start to display your products and signage. There's little to worry about in terms of how you will look. However, you will be very similar to all the other exhibitors. The decision you will have to make is whether to pay less for space only and then to spend the difference (and more) making yourself look unique.

It depends on what the cost difference between space only and shell scheme is of course and sometimes it isn't that much. There are a few things that you can do, however, to make even a shell scheme look a little different to all the other stands.

Every company erecting shell schemes for exhibition organisers will have a number of extras that you can select to make your stand work better for you. They will range from simple tables and chairs to built in cupboards and partitions. Take a good look at their catalogue since you may be able to add something to your stand for little additional cost which will make the show more effective for you.

*You may wish to play around with colours.* Every shell scheme stand is likely to be the same colour unless specified otherwise and most exhibitors won't go to the trouble of making any changes, so you can make your stand unique simply by choosing different colours. Maybe you can co-ordinate the stand with your company colours for very little extra cost?

Incidentally, if you have striking or different company colours, one of the measurements of just how high your profile has become is when people can guess who's stand it is just by seeing the basic stand without signage or company name displayed. **That's when you know that you have made an impression!**

## GOING MOBILE ...

It maybe that a shell scheme doesn't give you the flexibility that you need for your stand. If this is the case, rather than going for a purpose built stand which can cost large sums of money, you may wish to consider purchasing a mobile exhibition system which can be used time and time again. Lightweight, easy to erect and very effective in all types of exhibitions, there are lots of options to choose from and you can build up your system little by little as time goes by. Such a system is even more cost effective if you tend to attend a number of smaller shows where no stands are built for the exhibitors. *You can style your system with your company colours too.*

If you do decide to use your own system in an exhibition, make sure that you can still get carpeting laid on your space as sometimes it doesn't come with space only sites. However, you can simply rent your carpeting from the same company providing carpet for the show. A very simple but effective tip is to choose the same colour carpet for your stand as used for the aisles. This makes your stand look very much bigger as there is no natural break between the your space and the aisle. It also means that you may be able to sneak a few extra feet if you need it without it being noticed too much.

If you already have a mobile exhibition system and are using it inside a shell scheme at exhibitions you may be wasting your money. There is little point in renting a shell scheme and then covering up the walls with your own system. You can get all the facilities such as electricity to the stand without having a shell, so think about it and spend what you save on other aspects of the event.

There are other possibilities between the two options of shell or space only. You could have a half shell, half space stand, which will give you the option of a back wall to display your graphics, electrics and spotlights, but will also give you space at the front of the stand to demonstrate your products without having to negotiate supporting pillars. It can also be an answer if you have higher products but need a space which has a ceiling attached.

Pillars in exhibition halls can be a real problem, especially when you get to the hall and find that you have one right in the middle of your stand which you had overlooked on the plan. They can be a plus too since space which includes a pillar may be offered to you more cheaply. You can make a pillar a feature of your stand, using it to raise signs higher than you would normally be able to do, increasing the visibility of your stand.

The one item that really surprises first time exhibitors every time is the cost of getting electricity onto the stand. Unfortunately, in the larger shows, this service is provided by only one company and so if you want the product you have to pay the price. You aren't paying any more than anyone else and there's no way around it, so if you need electricity in the bigger halls, I'm afraid you are going to have to pay for it. The same applies to spotlights too, so the less you can get away with, the cheaper it will be.

## AND NOW FOR THE PRETTY BIT ...

Once you've chosen your space you will have to decide what you are going to display on the stand and how you can make it attractive to visitors.

This is when the creative mind can run wild and when you can be left with the most fantastic looking stand in the world ... *which just doesn't work to sell your product.*

At an exhibition I attended some time ago I spotted a very nicely designed stand which had a comfortable rest area built into it, presumably for chatting to customers after they had made their initial enquiry. Unfortunately, however, the only people using the rest area whilst drinking their coffee were the salespeople who should have been working on the stand but who were sitting around and watching the customers walk by!

In another exhibition hall there was a stand shaped like a box, with just one entry point. Inside the box were the products. The only problem was that the customers couldn't get in to see the products because the sales team, not wishing to stand in a *"box"*, were all standing at the entrance. Four *"six footers"* looking like a team of bouncers from the local nightclub!

The primary aims of any stand design must be to make it work for the salespeople using it and to attract visitors by displaying products most effectively. Everyone wants to have the best stand in the show and if, at the end of the day, your stand looks great and does an effective job too, then you will have achieved the best of both worlds. **However, many of the**

*Quick Tip*

Don't go mad with spotlights on your stand. Although they are important to display your products more effectively they can be very expensive. Also, if you specify a large number of spotlights on your stand, you'll find that it can become very warm indeed, making it uncomfortable for both staff and visitors alike. If you are intending to be at a lot of shows, you may want to consider purchasing your own spotlights and running them from your electricity supply.

**prettiest and most spectacular stands built at exhibitions have been designed to please the designer and not necessarily to sell the product.**

Just like many other areas covered in this book, stand design is a very specialised subject and best left in detail to the experts if you are looking to spend large amounts of money. However, there are a few general points that will help you to get the most out of your stand if you are designing it yourself. Firstly, try to keep in mind at all times the barriers that your potential customers may have to overcome to get onto your stand in the first place.

Exhibition visitors are happy to plod along around an exhibition, only stepping onto what they consider to be your territory when they have seen something that really makes it worth their while. They know that as soon as they step onto your stand they could be met by a hungry salesman, asking them questions and trying to sell them something. Anything that prevents them from moving out of their *"comfort zone"* (the aisle) will, therefore, be very effective.

One thing that may stop visitors stepping onto your stand is a step. *Yes, a simple step.* Even though it may be only two inches high it could be a three foot wall as far as some visitors are concerned. They view it as a very clear indication of areas. On the stand is your area and in the aisle is theirs. Apart from anything else, steps onto stands are very wheelchair and baby buggy unfriendly, something we should all be aware of.

The more that you close off your stand, just like in the example I gave earlier, the less the visitor will feel comfortable about stepping into your space. They will feel uncomfortable about browsing, realising that once they are caught on your stand they may find it difficult to get off. Yes, many potential customers see the stand as a spider's web which they aren't too keen to get sucked into.

Sometimes there's another group of people influencing the design of the stand who maybe shouldn't. *They are the salespeople working the show.* Don't get me wrong, when it comes to how best a product can be sold or demonstrated on a stand they should be listened to carefully. However, sometimes a stand is designed around how best the salespeople can get through the day after the excesses of the night before. Coffee making facilities, rest areas, coathooks and plenty of room for bags, cases and all the free gifts they can horde from other stands can become the main priorities, rather than the aims we have highlighted already.

**Exhibitions aren't fun,** they are hard work and you'll have to think about how best to treat your staff. We'll talk about that a little later. However, clearly, the only thing the stand should be built around is the product or service that you are offering.

## HITTING THEM BETWEEN THE EYES ...

Generally speaking, the message should be to keep it simple. You have very little time to make an impact when a visitor first glances at your stand - seconds almost, so you will want to make sure that in those few vital seconds you are able to form an image in your potential customers mind, one that will make him want to investigate further.

When you have a rough idea of the shape and the size of the stand, the next two elements to consider are the products and the graphics (or signage). Let's take the products first.

**Don't simply try to fill the space with as much product as you can.** You may feel that you have to have a lot of product around to justify the cost of the space, but, unless you are looking to sell off the stand and need the stock, you should limit your display to the few products you think will create the maximum interest. If not, you'll be in danger of making your overall message less clear.

If you find you have a lot of different products fighting for the same space on the stand a number of things happen. Firstly, your staff have a harder time working the stand as they will be constantly pulled from one product to the next by visitors interested in different things. This makes selling harder. Secondly, your potential customers may find it harder to

*Quick Tip*

Make sure that you have a secure area on any stand that you use. Exhibitions are great places to "lose" mobile 'phones, handbags and suchlike.

• • • • • • • • • • • • • • • • • •
**NOTES**

establish exactly what is the area of your expertise and, thirdly, and I see this happen a good deal, your potential customers cannot even get onto your stand properly because of the product laying around, filling every last foot of space!

**Your stand should be designed to make it very easy for visitors to get onto - and, once on, to be able to get off again when they are ready to leave.**

One of the easiest ways to make sure you have enough room on your stand to be able to *"work it"* properly is to plan the stand to scale and make cut-outs of the floor area taken up by the products you intend to display. By moving them about on your stand space you will get a good idea of where the best position is for each product. Believe me, there's nothing worse than going to an exhibition with no plan for your stand. You'll almost certainly waste hours, just moving what may be heavy items around, to make them fit the space you have been allocated. I've seen many examples of companies who have made no attempt to plan their stands having to make quick decisions about which item they are going to leave off because there was no room left.

Planning your stand right down to the last detail also means that you can be quite sure you have allocated enough space around each item so that customers can view the product comfortably and can be given a full demonstration if necessary without having to move around while you are showing various points that you wish to get across.

Whatever product you are taking to a show, for goodness sake make sure that the item is working before you get to the venue. There is nothing more frustrating than to find out that a product doesn't work or has a piece broken off on the morning of the show, so check each item carefully before you set off and check each item again when you have set it up on the stand. If you can carry spares with you do so and if you can't, at least have a plan in your own mind if the worse came to the worse - *because sometimes it will !*

### MAKING THE HEADLINES ...

Having made your decision about products on the stand, you now need to think about the graphics or signage you need to help to get your message across. Obviously you will want to feature the name of your company, but just as important is easy-to-display signage that will immediately attract your target customers and leave them in no doubt that they should step onto your stand and take a look at what you have to offer.

*A WALLFULL OF LEAFLETS WILL BE MESSY AND CONFUSING*

To make an impact don't make the visitor try to read lots of tiny signs or, even worse, a wall full of leaflets pinned up in no particular order. This is a common mistake amongst new exhibitors, usually due to the fact that they believe they don't have the budget to produce more professional material. Signage doesn't have to be expensive to look effective and can, if you treat it properly, be used time after time - so you'll get value for money.

*Quick Tip*
If you don't have signage and you only have leaflets to use to brighten up your stand walls, then try using a number of the same leaflet rather than many different ones. You may create a stronger effect.

If you want to make your stand look really unprofessional there's a very simple way to do it. First find any piece of paper that you can lay your hands on (it doesn't even have to be white - in fact a bit of old brown card is perfect), then, with a really thin pen that won't be able to be seen more than two feet away, scrawl your message in uneven letters. For good measure, add a spelling mistake or two. Now sit back and wait for all the show visitors to … *pass you by*. That may seem a little extreme, but you'll see businesses that have paid a substantial amount for their stand space use similar signs which, unfortunately, says more about the business than just the message on the sign itself. *So, do the job properly and look professional.*

As mentioned already, you'll have very little time to get your potential new customer interested in you, so why not try to read each of your signs in about five seconds flat from about six feet away. The chances are that you won't be able to, so why expect the visitors to? Pinning those leaflets to the back wall really is a waste of time, because no-one is going to get past the first sentence in a busy show.

**So, make the signage short and snappy.**

For example, if you are exhibiting a new range of pens that are smoother to write with and take less effort to use, you may want to focus on these features and benefits on the stand with a sign such as:

**You'll never use a smoother pen - try one !**

*Simple and effective.* Anyone in the market for a new pen (your target market) is at least going to have some interest in your product. The battle to capture the initial interest and pull the potential customer onto the stand has been won.

## FIND THE TRIGGER, FIND THE CUSTOMER …

In the sometimes hectic world of an exhibition, visitors are searching for keys to trigger their interest. In most cases they are looking for a solution to a particular problem that they may be facing or looking for an item which will improve some aspect of their lives. All you have to do is to find the trigger that will generate the interest and highlight it on your stand.

Just as we discussed in the section on direct mail, there are trigger words that will help you to attract visitors onto your stand. They are words such as:

*NEW*

*FREE*

*JUST ARRIVED*

*SPECIAL SHOW OFFER*

*DON'T MISS THIS*

*Quick Tip*

Attending an exhibition effectively means that you will have to allocate funds for a number of different but all the same important elements which, combined, will give you a professional image and help you to achieve results. Spend too much on one element and forget another and you will be missing out, so make sure that you budget sensibly for all the different aspects and that way you can be confident that you are approaching the promotion in the best way possible.

Most people are hoping to see something new when they visit an exhibition. In fact, for some visitors who may have persuaded their bosses to let them out of the office for the day, it is very important to find at least one new item so that they can justify their visit in their own minds before going back to the office. So, **NEW** is very important and can be the trigger which attracts a great many visitors to your stand.

**Think about the colours used for your signs too.** If you want your signs to stand out and shout your message loudly, then consider carefully which colours you should use for the background and for the actual lettering. Even if you aren't using a stand designer (and the chances are that you won't be), you can still ensure that you choose the correct combinations by playing around with a set of crayons and matching the colours to your stand background colour. You don't have to be an artist to do this and no-one but yourself is going to see the work, so scribble away and decide for yourself which colour combination suits your stand best.

The good news is that very simple signs on a smart but basic stand can be very effective. That's important not only to attract visitors but also for your staff who will feel better if they are working on a stand that looks good and feels good too.

As we've said, signage doesn't have to be expensive. There are always professional, value for money signwriters in every town, many of whom will have very advanced machinery and computer run equipment. The chances are that you will be able to get what you are looking for at the right price from one of these professionals. Use your local specialist to help out with advice about your signs too as they will have some valuable input. They can tell you what works and what doesn't.

As you attend more and more exhibitions you may wish to consider more advance signage for your stand, including rotating sign modules that can help to bring a little more life to an area, especially when the products are static or very difficult to demonstrate.

Following on from moving signage, just a short word about videos on exhibition stands. They can be very effective, especially if you want to show a special manufacturing technique that is impossible to display in other ways on the stand. The best videos for exhibition stands are the shortest. Some two to three minutes is long enough. Otherwise many visitors just won't take the time to see it through to the end. Remember the time pressures at a busy show .

If you do use a video, place it on the edge of the stand and use it to act as the hook to attract visitors. It will be wasted at the back of the stand unless you want to use it to talk more specifically in peace and quiet. Also try to make sure that the video is at eye level and not at a low level, making people bend down to watch it. At eye level, on its own stand maybe, the video has the opportunity to attract a crowd, just as a salesperson demonstrating a product would.

It is also a good idea to produce a sign to explain what the video is about. It can be very confusing in an exhibition hall when a number of things are going on to immediately focus in on a video and to realise that it is relevant for you, so a sign to get the message across will help to attract more people. If you are showing a new method of manufacturing the latest line of double glazed windows, for example, you might say:

### *LATEST TECHNIQUES MEAN*
### *LESS WINDOW DRAUGHT*

*Quick Tip*

Competitions can create interest on an exhibition stand. However, beware. Running a competition with no clear reason is only going to create a pile of low quality leads. Running a daily competition may be more effective at a longer show.

### ADDING INTEREST TO YOUR STAND ...

Should you run a special exhibition offer or other promotion at the show? An offer will attract visitors and can help you to monitor sales from the show, letting you form an opinion of its success.

Bear in mind though that sales can result quite a time after the exhibition in some cases. If you do decide to use an offer, then why not produce a special show leaflet giving you a single piece of information to distribute. If you are working on a stand there's nothing worse than having to handle 17 pieces of different literature which are probably all stored in a cupboard in no particular order.

If you aren't sure what type of offer you could run, why not take a trip out to another exhibition to see just what other companies are doing? It doesn't matter that they may not be in your industry or market, you'll be able to get plenty of ideas from the promotions you see. Going to other shows is a great way of learning more about how to and how not to approach exhibitions, so call one of the larger exhibition centres and find out what's on and make a date to drop in for some free training.

*CHAPTER 4*
# Making the stand really work for you

A number of different elements will combine to ensure that you enjoy an effective show. One of them is the use of literature.

How you use literature at an exhibition really depends on what type of event you are attending and what you are trying to achieve at the show. The two extremes are:

**A.** Give no information out at all or

**B.** Have all your literature on show for anyone to take as much as they wish.

Obviously there are also compromises too. Let's take the first option of having no literature on show for now.

If you wanted to have a reason to send your new contact details after the show you might decide to give nothing out on the day. By offering to send details of the product to the customer you generate something which is very valuable - *a name and address.* If you decide to take this approach then it is important to make sure that your staff can handle the enquiries properly and are effective at capturing the names and addresses. If you go down this route don't be tempted to take literature with you *"just in case",* because your staff will take the easy way out and you'll end up giving out the literature most of the time.

If you decide not to give details out, you will need to give the visitor a good reason why they can't take a leaflet with them. When asked for a product brochure you will need to say something like:

*" May I register you for our full information pack which we'll be sending to everyone straight after the show. That way we can give you all the details you need and we can include our special offers - plus, you don't have to carry it around with you all day long either!"*

You could decide to go part way and give the customer a teaser leaflet on the stand and then follow up with more detailed information a few days afterwards. A teaser leaflet gains the interest of the customer but doesn't offer too much information about the product or service you are selling. By giving something out on the stand, maybe with a special offer attached, you are able to satisfy the customer's need to take something away with them. However, giving out any piece of information is likely to reduce the percentage of personal details you secure as the customer sometimes takes the attitude that they'll come back to you if they need to.

*Make no mistake, getting personal details can be very difficult.* Most people don't want to have a follow-up. They haven't got the time and they don't need the hassle, so finding the right stand personnel to do the job is very important. A team member who is effective at getting the customers' details is worth their weight in gold in these circumstances.

Another option is to store all your literature on the stand but to have it out of sight, only to be given out by your stand personnel as and when they see fit. If you decide on this option

*Quick Tip*

If you are simply interested in getting as many names and addresses as possible at a show, to be able to follow up afterwards, then consider setting up a "registration point" where visitors can fill in their names and addresses, sometimes without even having to talk to a member of the stand staff. Signage such as "Catalogue Registration Point" may well be useful.

*Quick Tip*

When you are designing your stand, remember to consider your literature policy. You may wish to design a small secure area where you can display your brochures but where the visitors can't get at them. Having the brochures displayed properly for the sales team can save time and makes the stand easier to work.

then think about how you can ensure that the literature is kept tidy at all times. If it is a fast exhibition, it looks so inefficient if you are searching for five minutes for a particular leaflet.

Remember, just like anywhere else, first impressions count and even if the customer likes your product, the simplest thing such as keeping him waiting for information could mean that he doesn't consider your product at the end of the day. There are plenty of leaflet holders available in all shapes and sizes that you can attach to the walls of your stand and which will make everyone's life easier - think seriously about investing in a few for your next show.

Going the whole hog and having all your literature out on show is a great way of getting your message out and about. Unfortunately, if you are not careful, it is also a great way of loosing hundreds of pounds worth of leaflets with nothing to show for it when you get back to the office. Think very carefully before you display expensive colour brochures at the front of your stand for everyone to take whenever they wish. Having product information so readily available decreases the number of opportunities that you will get to talk properly to potential customers. What you will probably face is a response something like:

*Would you like any help Sir?*

*No thanks, I'll just take the brochures for now.*

All you have gained from that exchange is another set of brochures into the hands of a mystery contact. You just don't know who they are or where they are from and, unless they contact you to talk to you again, you are powerless to develop a possible sale further.

If you do want to have good quality product brochures displayed on your stand then at least place them at the back so that the customer has to get right onto your space to obtain details. This way, you have an opportunity to get a little more information out of them before they move off your stand.

### REDUCING THE WASTAGE ...

Just as in advertising, you are sure to experience some wastage at an exhibition and, as with advertising, the trick is to try to restrict the wastage to a minimum. Many people visit exhibitions and never buy anything from anyone, either at the show or afterwards. They are just *"interested"*. You also get a fair number of schoolchildren and students who may be doing projects or have just been brought out for the day. These are the types of visitors you have to watch carefully if you are displaying your brochures for all to see.

This is one reason why you may wish to print a special leaflet just for the exhibition, to focus more clearly on the message that you wish to get over and, at the same time, to ensure that your more expensive quality literature is used wisely. An investment in a single colour, one sided leaflet may well save you money in the future and will give you a larger quantity of leaflets to use and an improved chance of more extensive coverage.

Whatever you are handing out at an exhibition, it makes sense to use a coupon so that you have a chance, at least, of getting replies after the show. This is especially useful if you

*Quick Tip*

Getting literature on display at the entrance to the show can give you an excellent route to get your message across. If you can do this free of charge even better. However, you may have to pay for the privilege, but, if it's a busy show, it may well be worth it. The literature given out should be low cost with a coupon for response.

are attending a show where the visitors may be travelling some distance, since they may be more likely to send off for further details by mail rather than calling you if they have the choice. Giving out any information without a strong *"call to action"* such as a bold phone number or a coupon will dramatically reduce the results you see in the weeks or months after the show.

Pro-actively seeking out the customer by being at the entrance to the show and giving out your brochures is one way to make an impact. You'll probably have to get permission to do this. If there's a queuing system at the entrance, simply walking down the line with a cheery *"Good Morning"* as you hand out your literature is a good way to get the information out. Catching the customer while they are waiting to register may be just the time to get your message across.

The final advice regarding literature at exhibitions is to consider making it a different size. Usually there are lots of exhibitors trying to get as much information off their stands and into the hands of the visitors as possible and they all generally use either A4 or A5 literature sizes. When the visitor returns home and unpacks all the information it all tends to look the same. If you choose an odd size, then at least your information is going to stand out from the crowd and that will give it just that little extra help it may need to be picked up and read once again. Using a striking colour can also help to "lift" your information above all the other leaflets competing for attention.

DOUBLE
BAGGER

## BEWARE THE DOUBLE BAGGER ...

Keep your eye out for the *"double bagger"*. This is a term used by exhibitors to label the visitor who is just "interested" but intent on collecting information on every product off every stand. You'll see them approaching your stand with, of course, two or more bagfuls of product literature. From the moment they get into the exhibition, to the moment they leave they are dashing about from one stand to the next picking up every piece of literature that they can get their hands on. And what will they do with it?

Well, generally they will take it back to the office or to their home and it will sit in the bags for days or maybe weeks. If you are lucky it may get looked through briefly but then discarded. Unfortunately it is more likely that by the time the *"Double Bagger"* has found a few minutes to look through the mass of information he or she has collected, they have forgotten why they picked most of it up, lost interest or just cannot be bothered to wade through it all. They have probably walked out of the exhibition with over £50 worth of literature - maybe a considerable amount more and now they are about to dump it all in the bin. *Sad isn't it?*

*Beware the "Double Bagger"!*

Having said that, literature can be a useful tool to move people off your stand. If you know that the person you have been lumbered with for the past 20 minutes isn't going to buy a product from you, however long you stand chatting to them, then giving them the full set of literature to get them off your stand so that you can concentrate on a real customer may be the most sensible and cost effective thing to do. In fast moving exhibitions you can-

*Quick Tip*

A slightly naughty, but fun way to gain added exposure at a show is to page members of staff on the show tannoy throughout the day. Asking for Tony to go to the "Griffins Stand" is one way of getting your name out and about !!

not afford to get stuck with a timewaster as they may cause you to miss a number of better quality contacts while you are tied up.

### DOING THE BUSINESS ON THE STAND ...

Once the customer is on your stand they need to be taken care of in a professional manner, given all the details about the product and, if appropriate, given a demonstration. *If you are really lucky they may be asked to buy a product and even say yes!!*

It is important to recognise that once you have done the work to get a potential customer onto your stand with your stand design and product range, you risk making your results less effective by not taking care to ensure that your staff are fully equipped to deal with enquiries and to sell the product properly.

"NO THANKS — JUST LOOKING...."

### BEING BETTER EQUIPPED TO SELL.....

Here's a few simple observations that may make your exhibition a little more effective. Firstly, how many times have you stepped onto an exhibition stand only to hear the words *"Can I help you, Sir?"* I'm sure that you've heard this line many times - not only at exhibitions but also in shops of all kinds. Your answer to such a question is generally *"No thanks, I'm just looking"*.

An exhibition is full of people *"just looking"*. They may *"just look"* at your product but buy a similar one around the corner. So how do you make sure that when you have a potential customer on the stand you give yourself the best chance possible of getting a result? Selling is an art and training is required to make people more effective. Nevertheless, if you don't do anything else with your staff, then make sure that they approach the customer with

"Good Morning, Sir. What are you particularly interested in ?"

an *"Open Question"* (i.e. one that requires an answer other than yes or no). Such a question could be something like :

- ***Good morning Sir, what are you particularly interested in? or***

- ***Which particular product has caught your eye today?***

At least using this approach you have half a chance of having a proper conversation with the potential customer and finding out more about his or her needs.

Exhibition visitors appreciate professional selling but don't want to be pressurised into buying a product. That's why that awful question *"Can I help you?"* gets such a negative reply. It reminds us of the teenage assistant in the clothes shop who has been told to ask the question to every customer who walks through the door regardless.

So, don't pester, don't pounce, but be professional and draw the visitor into a conversation. One method of achieving this is to canvass the visitor. Ask them a couple of questions to find out if they already purchase products like yours and, if so, who they buy from at present.

This method of engaging the customer is sometimes known as **"Kissing Frogs"**, because you have to talk to a lot visitors before you find a prospect you can sell to.

This *"Pro-active"* style of interacting with visitors may not be to your liking or to the liking of your staff. Maybe you wouldn't feel comfortable doing it. That's OK, it's a case of horses for courses, but maybe you might consider employing specialist promotional staff who can do that job for you.

There isn't much point in spending good money attending a show if neither yourself nor your staff are equipped to be able to get the necessary results. If you aren't confident of your ability consider hiring a specialist to be on your stand who is use to *"working"* an exhibition and talking to potential customers.

You may find that you can use one of these specialists to do all the canvassing work while your own staff take over when the initial contact has been made. If you hire a good front line person, then both yourself and your staff will be able to watch and learn so that, in future, you may not have to go outside for help. You will find companies specialising in exhibition staff in Yellow Pages under either *"promotions"* or *"exhibitions"*.

Just as each person has their own particular job to do in their normal workplace, you may find that you want to specialise on your exhibition stand. The fact is that some people are better at certain tasks than others, wherever they are. If you have a good salesperson who is great at closing the sale one to one, but hates cold calling, then make sure he is *"fed"* customers by someone else who may be better at building a relationship quickly with a stranger.

If you have a large enough stand you can even design around this principle, with the front part of the stand used to make the initial contact and the rear of the stand used as a quieter area, to create the right atmosphere for the sale to be made.

A stand I once saw in a major exhibition incorporated this style and was very effective. An island site, the stand had three distinct sections. The outer section was manned by the first set of team members whose job it was to make contact with the customer. This they would do using a *"pro-active"* approach, sometimes even just by looking at the visitor and making strong eye contact. Once they had *"engaged"* the customer and had got them interested in the product they were selling (with the aid of a free offer and prize draw), they drew them into the second section where they sat the customer down at a table and talked some more.

When they had finally reached the stage of closing the sale, they moved the customer into a third stage where they were signed up by another team member. What they were actually doing with the customer was moving them further into *"their"* space and getting them more committed little by little. By drawing them, using small steps, into the body of their stand, they were almost pulling the customer in like a fly into a spider's web. *Very clever.*

NOTES

*Quick Tip*

The right team at the exhibition can be very effective. However, picking the wrong combination of people to work closely together on a stand can be very detrimental, both during the show and afterwards for months to come, so choose wisely.

That might seem a rather overcomplicated method and most readers will not have resources to build what was a rather complex and clever stand - not just yet anyway! However, the principle is the same whether you are on a 2 sq. metre or 200 sq. metre stand. It boils down to finding ideas that work and using them to your best advantage. When you go to another exhibition to look for inspiration, then these are just some of the things that you should be aware of and take a note of for future use:

- Effective stand designs that look as though they are working well.

- Effective signage that really stands out and gets noticed.

- Methods of approach used to get you on the stand.

- Special offers that are attracting interest.

- Any unusual free gifts.

- Original literature displays.

- Team uniforms that caught the eye.

- The best use of the smallest space.

### A WORD IN THE RIGHT EAR ...

Before you attend an exhibition take time to brief all the staff you intend to use as a part of your team. They will need to know about the main selling features and benefits of the products on display and any offers that may be run during the exhibition. If possible have a meeting before you get to the exhibition, to run through the main aims of the show and to make sure that you emphasise the most important points that you want your staff to keep in mind.

It's also a good idea to have a stand meeting on the first morning of the show to reiterate the aims of the exhibition, ensure that any questions are fully answered and to give the team a chance to get to know the stand and how it's put together. Naturally, this is more important if the stand is of some size.

**Oh, and tell your staff how much the show has cost to attend - that tends to focus the mind, especially if it is an expensive show to be at!**

Either the night before or the morning of the show is also the time to motivate your team, however small, and to build the team spirit that will be needed to see you through a longer exhibition. Contrary to the opinion held by the staff back at the office, exhibitions are hard work, both mentally and physically, and to get the most from your stand staff you will need to reward their efforts with pats on the back, a special meal or even cash incentives. If you manage your team properly you will have an effective selling force at the show and will be rewarded with real results to take away with you. If not, you may be left with very tired, disgruntled staff who will troop back to the office with sad and gruesome tales, bringing everyone down along the way.

**If you can, try to ensure that you or a member of your staff never attend an important exhibition alone.** If you are spending considerable sums of money to attend an exhibition, spend a little more to ensure that staffing levels on the stand are correct, even if it means someone simply covering the lunchtime period to give another staff member a break. There's nothing worse and sadly ineffective than a stand left unattended for even a few minutes while a potential buyer tries in vain to get some attention or help. Remember, the one you miss might just be the one that could have made the whole exhibition worthwhile.

### THE RIGHT TOOLS TO DO THE JOB ...

One of the most important and yet simplest aids that you can provide your team is an effective enquiry form to use on the stand. One of the most frustrating results from any show is when you are told that you have had *"lots of people"* interested in your products but, at the end of the day, you have very few names and addresses to follow up when you are back in the office. If you have worked hard to get visitors onto your stand don't let them get away without at least getting their details.

Each enquiry form will be different of course, but the basics are name and address, telephone number, products of interest etc. After that you can incorporate a number of other questions to help you find out more about your prospect. You can even design the form to work as a guide for your staff, taking them through a simple sales pitch if necessary. But, beware, don't make the form too long - visitors generally like to get on and off the stand as quickly as possible.

**If you want to provide an incentive for your staff, why not give a prize for the most enquiries taken at the show - but only count those that are filled in completely and correctly.**

### THE BEST DRESSED TEAM IN TOWN ...

*You may want to consider uniforms for your exhibition team.* Uniforms can vary from a simple sweater with logo to a smart suit and it really is a matter of personal taste and how you see your own company image. It also depends on the type of customer that you are dealing with. Some customers will feel a lot more comfortable talking to casually dressed salespeople while others may believe that business should be carried out in a more formal dress code. It also depends on what your team feel comfortable in too. Uniforms, or at least similar dress codes, have a number of advantages though:

- They make it easier for the visitors to identify the members of your team. Especially useful at busier exhibitions.

- They identify your team members to other companies attending the show, useful if you are in an Industry show and are looking to establish or reinforce an image.

- They build team spirit (the one for all and all for one attitude).

- Depending on the style you choose, they can be more comfortable for a long day on the stand.

Your staff are almost certain to have their own views on uniforms and they should be listened to as they are the ones who will be wearing them. However, if you feel it is right for you, then don't back down if one member of staff isn't keen. *Lead the way by wearing it yourself if necessary.* Depending on the type of show you are attending, you don't have to be so subtle. If you want to print your company name big and bold on the back of your sweatshirts - do so. Anything that gets across your name and builds your awareness should be considered seriously.

**Along with uniforms you will most certainly want to consider name badges.** Name badges also help to identify the members of the team and, to some extent, help to build the relationship between salesperson and customer since at least they know your name before they make verbal contact. Badges should be clear and easy to read and preferably printed with your logo on them. Remember, at an exhibition one of the objectives has to be to get your company name in front of the visitors as many times as possible, so that you have a better chance of them remembering it. Having your logo on the badges gives you endless opportunities to get your name in front of the customers.

*CHAPTER 5*
# The nuts and bolts of attending a show

Let's now move on and look at the nuts and bolts of attending an exhibition. First of all, if you have the opportunity, make sure that you set up your stand the day before the show begins. Most shows will give you this set-up time. Trying to set up your stand the day of an exhibition when the show opens at 10.00am and you don't get into the hall until 9.15am is

**NOTES**

*Quick Tip*

Providing plastic bags can be a great way to increase your visibility in a show. Having 2,000 people walking around with your logo on their bag is quite powerful. If you can, try to place the bags at the entrances to the show. That way visitors will pick up your bag first. Plastic bags can hang around a very long time both in the office and at your customer's home.

*Quick Tip*

If you are intending to give out leaflets along with your business card, remember to take a stapler with you to use on the stand, otherwise your card will get separated and probably lost in the mass of information collected on the day.

• • • • • • • • • • • • • • • • • •

**NOTES**

no joke I assure you. You'll be rushed and your display simply won't be as effective as it could have been. *If you are spending money attending a show, then try to get the most out of it.*

No matter what sized stand, whatever you do, when you arrive in the exhibition hall and have found your space don't unload your products directly onto your stand if you can avoid doing so. If you do make this mistake you'll find that when you've unloaded all your products, literature, furniture and other display material neatly into your allocated area, you'll have to take it all off again when you start to set the stand up properly!

This is another good reason for setting up your stand nice and early, as you can use the stand next door to store your products and stand materials until you need them. So, start off with a clean, clear stand and build it up little by little. That way, hopefully, you'll only have to do the job once and you won't find yourself moving the same items around and around all day long, trying to create space.

The day before an exhibition can be used not only to get your stand in order but also to get to know the exhibition a little better. Or, if you know the exhibition well, you can use the time to talk to colleagues, competitors and new companies that you may be unaware of. If you are attending a busy exhibition and you don't have the luxury of large numbers of staff to man the stand, you may end up seeing nothing of the show yourself during opening hours, so set-up day can be a good time to take a look at who's doing what.

Giving yourself this breathing space also allows you the time to react to competitive situations. For example, if a competitor has a special deal that is likely to cause you a problem during the show, then you still have the time to revise your own plans, get new signage produced if you need to and brief your team before the show opens. You can't do that so easily if you only have a few minutes to react to the news, or, even worse, if you only find out from visitors to your stand during the show itself.

On the subject of special offers, if you have an offer that you hope will take the wind out of a competitor's sails, then don't display it before the opening of the show. If you do it will only give them time to react if they are about, walking around and checking out the market before the show opens.

If you haven't yet attended an exhibition, you'll be amazed just how long it can take to set up a stand properly. *The key word here is "properly" of course.* It doesn't take too long to find an area and dump some products, find a chair and sit by them, but it can take a while to do the job effectively. Give yourself plenty of time and then add another hour or two - *the chances are you'll need them.*

My own preference when setting up a stand is to get the signage right first, simply because it can be such an important element of the stand's success. Forget the products for a while and concentrate on getting the messages clearly seen from all angles. It drives me crazy when I see stands which have signs, posters and photographs displayed at different levels or even at an angle - it looks so unprofessional.

When you are confident that the signage is right, then arrange the product display if you have one. Remember to test out whether it will work for your visitors by making sure that they can get around the stand easily. Remember also to test the products to make sure they are still working too.

Literature placement would be the next thing to organise and at this stage you would want to make up any packs you are considering giving out so that you have some ready for the opening. Whoever has been selected for the task of setting up should remember that their job is make the stand as ready as possible for the other team members, who may only arrive on the morning of the show. Every little detail should be taken care of, so that the salespeople can arrive, take off their coats, get to know the stand for a few minutes and be able to greet prospective customers with confidence.

**Making sure that the stand is ready for a long day's work doesn't just apply on the**

*Quick Tip*

When the show is underway, take a few minutes to stand back and take a look at how the stand is working. Are the products placed in the right positions? Are the staff able to "work" the stand properly? If you see something that isn't working, don't be afraid to change it during the show.

**first day of the show.** If you are attending a show of two or three days' duration you will want to ensure that the stand is looking as good on day three as it did on day one. Sometimes companies forget this and their space looks untidy, messy and even dirty on the second day of the show. It's as though they think that as long as they look all right for the opening, that's the job done.

*It isn't of course.* Full and overflowing waste baskets with the remains of the previous day's sandwiches, literature racks that no-one could possibly find the right brochures on and products that have more finger marks on them than a police burglary exhibit isn't going to impress the customer greatly. Make sure that someone is designated and accepted as stand manager for the show and that they understand it is their task to ensure that the stand is in good working order at least half an hour before the doors open to visitors each day. Whether they do it themselves or they delegate specific tasks is entirely up to them - *as long as the jobs get done.*

## AT THE END OF THE SHOW ...

An hour before a show closes, maybe a lot sooner if it has been a quiet show, the exhibitors will become restless. Small parts of each stand will start to disappear in a miraculous way. Graphics will suddenly vanish from the back of the stand, the odd product will find its way into a van and literature will be boxed, ready for the off. This is only natural, especially if it has been a long two or three days. People want to get home. However, beware as this is the time that you can end up wasting a good deal of money, just for the sake of taking your time a little more. Graphics, signage and photographs can be expensive and you don't want to end up paying for their use at just one show.

**Emphasise to the people involved at the end of the show the need for care.** Being careful enough to save the protective wrappings and boxes which were used to bring the items to the show can make all the difference. Remembering these small points will save you money and reduce the frustration you'll feel when you see once perfect signs ripped and battered, laying in the corner of a dirty warehouse, never able to be used again.

On the subject of maintaining signage etc in good order, spending a little more initially may ensure that you get more for your money in the long run. Having signs produced on cardboard or paper is fine if you are looking for a *"one off"* use. However, if you are planning to use them time and time again, then spend more and have them produced on a better quality, stronger material. However hard you try, you'll find it very difficult to protect cardboard signs unless you have them laminated. Edges get torn and corners get knocked. A harder, more durable material will cost more but save you money eventually. Your local signmaker will be able to advise you on the types of material available.

*CHAPTER 6*
# Reaping the rewards of your efforts

The show is over. Everyone is back in the office. The tales of late night drinking and the amazing mixture of different cuisines enjoyed have done the rounds and there isn't much left to show for the experience ... *not much that is, apart from a pile of enquiry forms sitting on a desk waiting for someone to action them.*

Amazingly enough, some companies are content to attend an exhibition, spend large sums of money on the stand and the display and then completely ignore the fruits of their labours once they get back into the familiar office routine. Maybe they think that the customer will be phoning them, pleading to allow them to place a huge order, or maybe they think that the enquiries aren't worth the effort.

**The very first task when you return from an exhibition should be to put into action a plan drawn up before the show commenced.**

Potential customers need following up quickly, within days if possible. The longer you

*Action Point*

Make a note in your diary to review all the leads generated at an exhibition three months after the show. If necessary, if selling times are longer, make another date at that time to review them again. This is the only sure way of knowing whether what you created has been converted into business.

leave the follow-up the less effective it will be, it's as simple as that. The customers have been on your stand, have looked at your products and have expressed an interest. *They are hot leads.* Leave them for a few weeks, maybe even a month, and you might just as well be mailing them completely cold for all the effect your time with them at the show will have had.

Because everyday problems and daily routines will have piled up while you were away, you'll need to be very disciplined to get the most from the enquiries generated. Put aside a day, two days or however long it takes to make sure the job is done and done properly. Do nothing else during this time. It's hard but necessary if you are to get the most from the show.

Before attending the show you should have sat down and thought about what information to send potential customers afterwards. This information could even be pre-packed to make it easier for you when you return. Receiving information only a day or two after talking to someone on an exhibition stand is very powerful. *It absolutely stinks of efficiency.*

If you generate a lot of enquiries, then you may consider sending them back to the office each evening to be dealt with the following day. This way you won't be faced with hundreds of information packs to send on your return. Also, each of your potential customers will receive their information a day or two earlier. If they are away from the office for a few days, you may even have the pack sitting on their desk the moment they get back to their desk - that's impressive.

Make sure you collect all the enquiries back at the office. Sometimes there is a temptation to pass out enquiries to salespeople on the stand, leaving them to action follow-ups themselves. ***Don't.*** You'll want to have all the enquiries under your control where you can follow their progress - it's the only way to monitor the true performance of the exhibition and, of course, the salespeople.

When you send information to contacts made at the show, make sure that they can identify with the package. They will most probably have talked to a number of different companies and might not remember exactly what you had to offer, so remind them. Thank them for visiting your stand and try to paint a picture of your exhibit. You may even wish to send them a photograph of your stand, just to jog the memory further. Just as when you are sending information to a *"cold"* contact using direct mail, you'll need to make sure they know what they are expected to do next, i.e. are you calling them or do they need to call you?

**Action Point**

Before you attend an exhibition, list the types of questions that you feel will help to identify real potential customers.

## WEEDING OUT THE RUBBISH ...

Whenever you return from a reasonably busy exhibition and if you are lucky you'll probably have generated too many enquiries to be able to follow up properly quickly. One way of trying to manage this problem is to identify enquiries which should be given priority.

The only real way to do this effectively is to make a judgement on the stand just after you have finished talking to the prospect. A simple but useful method of selection is for you and your staff to mark each enquiry form with a grading which can be used back at the office. For example, you might employ a scale of 1 to 6. Anyone graded as category 1 is, in the opinion of the team member who made contact, an excellent prospect and one who should be given priority when it comes to a follow-up. Anyone marked as a 6 will have been classified as having less potential.

This system of grading means that anyone picking up the leads, even not having attended the exhibition, can sort them into priority and will have a starting point. Without some sort of classification you only have a bunch of leads which all seem the same. Even if notes have been written on the lead forms, it is very difficult to remember the quality of each contact a few days after the show.

Clearly the grading will be more precise depending on the quality of questions asked. It is possible to weed out the timewasters and those visitors who just don't have the power to make any kind of decision by asking the right questions.

## CLOSING THE SHOW ...

Finally, when you have returned to the office, try to take a few minutes to collect your thoughts on the show. Although you might not know for some time whether it has been truly effective, you will be able to put down on paper what worked and what didn't. If you intend to exhibit again at a similar show, then the ideas and thoughts you have now will come in useful for sure.

*Make time to discuss the show with the staff who were on the stand too.* Don't wait for a slack moment three weeks later or at the end of the next sales meeting the following month. If you leave it you'll get very little feedback because most of the good points which could have be discussed and actioned will have either been forgotten completely or people's judgements will be less clear.

Whatever ideas, suggestions and comments result, place them in the exhibition file or in a bring forward file if you use one, so that they are handy the next time you exhibit. That way you won't end up making the same mistakes time after time.

Exhibiting can be very cost effective and it can be a real waste of time and effort. Sometimes it depends on the show you are attending, but more often than not it will be down to planning. Make every effort to have a good show and the chances are that you will be pleased with the results. Think that you can simply turn up on the day and you'll need a pretty exceptional product to carry you through. ***The choice is yours.***

---

## Summary Points

1. Make sure you have a good reason to attend each show.

2. Always try to book the most effective spaces in the hall.

3. Spend time thinking about your stand design, don't clutter it up with either too many products or too much information.

4. Have a literature strategy. Know exactly what you are giving out and why.

5. Spend time making sure that any staff working the stand have been trained both in the products and how to deal with visitors.

6. After the show is over, concentrate on the enquiries you have generated. Make the most of the leads you have produced.

---

*SECTION FIVE*

# Always being one step in front of the competition

## CHAPTER 1
# Understanding the power of being the best

This section is devoted to looking good and feeling good. Everything you have read already will be worth very little unless you can be sure that your customers feel good about doing business with you. Spending thousands on a new advertising campaign, mailing hundreds of new potential customers, taking the time to develop an ongoing PR programme could all be worthless if the moment the customer comes into contact with your company you perform like a third rate cowboy outfit.

I make no apologies about adding a chapter about becoming the best. I feel it's just as much a part of marketing as any other tool we have highlighted so far. The next few pages are just a few ideas to get you thinking.

Making sure that you look good in print or at an exhibition is just part of the battle that you must win if you want to keep the customers you have already and at the same time enlarge the numbers of new customers you welcome into your business each day.

Taking some of the steps that you have already read about will make a difference, but when you are implementing any new marketing initiative you'll want to be sure that all the good work isn't wasted the first time the potential customer makes contact with you. Ensuring that every time a customer comes into contact with your company they are impressed with the quality of care and service offered has to be a major aim of anyone serious about building their business in the face of growing competition.

There have been a number of books written on **"excellence"** over the past few years. You may be able to think of a number of companies at the forefront of the *"excellence"* approach. However, there are also companies in business today almost in spite of themselves, companies that don't seem to care too much about the customer.

### WHICH TYPE OF COMPANY IS YOURS? ...

Some time ago, on my father's birthday, my parents were going out for dinner to celebrate. They live some 70 miles away from me. I had decided that I would like to pay for their dinner that evening and so I discovered where they were intending to eat and gave the restaurant a call the night before.

I told the manager what I would like to do and he said that it would be no problem - they wouldn't give my parents a bill but would simply use my credit card number which I had given to them to pay for the meal.

My parents were due to arrive at the restaurant at 7.30pm. At 9.00pm I received a call, full of apologies. There had been a mistake and my parents had somehow managed to pay their own bill. They had left the restaurant to return home. Apparently, there was a new member of staff serving that night and somehow the message hadn't got through to him.

I was disappointed, and, for a moment, a little upset that they had let the problem occur, but after accepting sincere apologies from the head waiter I forgot about the incident and went back to watching television.

Just 10 minutes later my viewing was interrupted once again by another telephone call, this time from the manager of the restaurant. He told me that he too was very sorry that they had managed to mess things up and he felt really bad about it. So bad in fact that he had 'phoned the restaurant owner, who happened to be at home at the time, and told him of the mistake. He continued to inform me that he was about to take the cost of the meal round to my parents' house along with a voucher for a free meal and bottle of champagne which they could use on their next visit. *Was that all right?*

Sure enough about 15 minutes later I received a call from my parents, surprised that they had been given their money back for a meal they had just eaten along with a voucher to do it all over again on the house!!

**That is an example of treating the customer right. That is excellence in action.**

Ask yourself what you would have done in the manager's position. If you find yourself considering for one moment the cost to the company just think of all the people that I, my parents and their friends have told the story to. *Each time that ordinary restaurant becomes something rather special indeed.*

The manager knew what he was doing. He was building customers for the future. He was giving service that was so special that it would get noticed in a big way.

But you don't have to give over the top service to look great these days. Simply getting the little things right will make a huge difference and put you right out in front.

## A HORROR STORY ...

I bought the computer on which I am writing this book from a major retail chain. I had problems getting the printer to work properly. However, each time I tried to speak to the salesman who had sold me the product he wasn't available. I left messages but he never rang back. I was getting very irritated by now. I visited the store and spoke to a number of people who didn't seem to know anything about the product they were selling. What's more, they didn't have another product to exchange because the item was now de-stocked.

Finally, after three weeks of frustration, I managed to get hold of the manager, but only by visiting the store which was some miles from my home. He was a nice enough guy but his hands were tied by Head Office. He had to follow a painfully slow procedure.

**Does this story sound familiar to you?**

I eventually got my problem sorted out, but the point was that I, the customer, was the one doing all the running around, all the pushing and shoving to get the problem solved. *Quite frankly it seemed as though they really didn't want to know once they had sold me the product and taken my money.*

The final nail in the coffin came when a replacement ink cartridge, promised to me at the time of the sale didn't show up, even after a number of 'phone calls. I received it some six weeks late!

**I won't be going back** - and, what's more, whenever someone mentions their name I take great delight in telling them why they should chose somewhere else to shop. I must have lost them thousands of pounds worth of business so far!

*You see, I'm an ordinary customer.* You mess me about and I'll get my own back in the end. How many ex-customers do you have running around telling everyone they meet not to buy from you? Or are you different? Are you lucky enough to have customers helping you with your marketing, extolling your virtues to everyone they come across?

*Action Point*
Do you have a complaints procedure to deal with problems as they arise? If you have staff, do they know what the procedure is ? If you do have a procedure in place, is it fair and does it work?

## *CHAPTER 2*
# Learning to stand out from the crowd ...

How can you make an impression? How can you stand out from the crowd in a competitive market place? The answer is really amazingly simple. Start with the little things, the things that we all take for granted, the things that matter when the customer comes into contact with your company for the very first time.

Whether you are the Owner or Managing Director of a company employing hundreds of people or you are working out of your bedroom, it's most probable that you will have customers calling you on the telephone. *How do you answer the telephone?*

It's a simple enough question, but do you or your staff actually know how they should be answering the 'phone? Do you have an efficient receptionist who is on first name terms with every one of your customers or does your telephone manner sound more like the customer is interrupting your day when they call? The fact is that on many occasions there are no guidelines published to show what is required when the telephone is answered and that's a shame because it's generally the single most important point of contact for your customers and one where you can score over your competitors heavily without much effort.

In a small company where everyone answers the telephone it's even more important to establish a telephone culture and to get the message across that you're an efficient company with which to do business. The message to the customer must be that *"we're really pleased that you've called us today".*

*Just think about it for a moment.* You must be able to remember occasions when you have contacted a company by 'phone only to hear an unprofessional answer when the telephone is eventually picked up. How does your own company sound? Do you ever telephone your own company to find out how your customers are being greeted?

Telephoning your competition will give you a good idea about how they view the customer and show you just how much better than them you can be. On the other hand it may show you just how much you have to improve to be as good as them.

Generally a pleasant *"Good Morning"* or *"Good Afternoon"* helps to start the ball rolling. This may seem elementary, but how many times have you telephoned a company only to hear *"Yes"*, or just as bad *"745678"*. When this happens you think that you have phoned the wrong number and respond by saying something like *"Oh, is that DJ Plumbing Services?"*

**Never be afraid to give out the company name big and bold**, after all it's all free advertising and every time the customer hears it you can be sure the awareness levels are rising. After the greeting and company name the next stage is to give out your own name to build personal contact with the caller. After this has been achieved we can then ask how we can help. Receiving a call may sound like …

**"Good Morning, J & J Lighting Services, Joanne speaking, how can I help you?"**

You'll be surprised how many customers will answer by saying something like:

*"Oh, hello Joanne …"* When that starts to happen the company is already forming a relationship with the potential customer, even after the first few seconds.

In some companies, you can be passed through numerous departments before you finally get an answer to a question you have asked and still no-one will have offered you their name. It's almost as though employees are frightened to be identified. Maybe they're ashamed of working for the company. It follows that no real contact is made. No wonder the customer feels that he or she is dealing with a faceless animal.

Face to face contact is just as important as the telephone when looking to make the right first impression. As we have already mentioned in the section on exhibitions, it's that crucial first few seconds that will make the difference.

If you work in a retail environment then, clearly, this is even more important. Everyone in your organisation has the power to either lose or gain a customer - a customer who may return again and again and again. Treating the customer as though they are the most important person in the world is easy on paper but sometimes a little more difficult in practise .

As most of us are aware, when you're trying to serve two or three people at the same time, the 'phone is ringing and the postman has arrived to collect that special parcel that has to be delivered the next day, the concept of customer care can go out the window - *along with the sales!*

Although sometimes incredibly difficult, it's crucial to understand that dealing with the customer is the most important thing you have to do - no matter what other tasks are also crying out for your attention. If you find yourself in the situation described above, then clearly you are going to be under some pressure to get the job done to everyone's satisfaction. However, simply informing the customer what is happening is sometimes all that is required to keep them happy while you work to get other things sorted out so that you can give them your full attention.

**It happens all the time.** You telephone a company and right in the middle of explaining the reason for your call you are transferred to a different department where you are expected to start all over again - transferred without even an explanation. Do you find this frustrating? Of course you do and if you are doing it to your own customers then they are finding it frustrating too.

"*I DO HOPE WE HAVEN'T KEPT YOU TOO LONG !*"

## INFORMATION IS THE KEY ...

*How about this.* You enter a shop to buy a certain item. You talk to the salesperson. Suddenly, he disappears and doesn't come back. Five minutes later you are still stood in the middle of the shop looking lost and there's no salesperson in sight. In fact he's trying to locate a product from another store and is on the telephone. The only problem is that he has not told you what he is trying to do for you and so you're getting more and more frustrated and angry that you have been left alone. You think that you are being ignored, when the reality is that the salesperson is doing everything he can for you.

*Quick Tip*
Always try to see your business through your customers eyes

If the salesperson had told you what he was about to do before disappearing, you would have been a lot happier. In fact, instead of standing, fuming, thinking of how you were going to tear a piece off him when he came back, or, even worse, walking out the door and vowing never to come back again, you may well take a relaxing walk around the store, browsing at other products on display and might even find something else to spend your money on while you're waiting. **It's easy, just keep the customer informed about what is going on and what you are doing to help.**

One example of keeping the customer informed happened to me at a lunch I was attending with 200 other guests. One of the main speakers was late and the invited guests were getting rather restless. You can image the comments about the organisers and the speaker as it became later and later, and hungry businessmen were forced to spend more time than they would have wished at an expensive pre-lunch bar. Finally the guest arrived and the lunch began. When it came to the turn of the speaker who had held up proceedings to say a few words you could almost hear the mumblings of derogatory comments that were being whispered around the tables - that is until the gentleman introducing the speaker informed us that he had rushed over to be with us today ... straight from his daughter's wedding reception!!

If the guests had been told the reason for the late arrival they would have quite happily waited, even for much longer than they actually did, but no-one told them why they were hanging about and they assumed the worst. Sometimes it isn't what you know but when you know it.

Face to face or on the telephone, even when you write to the customer, if you tell them what you are doing and why you are doing it you stand a much better chance of being understood and of getting a reputation for looking after your customers' needs. Unfortunately, these days, business seems to be so fast that unless you are running at 100 miles an hour you have the feeling that you are going backwards. It is hard to step back and

• • • • • • • • • • • • • • • • • • •

**NOTES**

take time with customers, but the fact is that the more time you spend with the customer, the more your reputation will build.

**Although using the telephone properly should be so simple, it doesn't happen in many, many organisations.** As the telephone is one of the very first experiences a potential customer may have with your company, it's worth spending a little time on getting it right. Training your staff, even for a few minutes, on how to handle the types of calls your company receives will bring its rewards in the future for sure.

So many times, new receptionists and other office staff who are expected to answer the telephone and become your very own public relations consultants are thrown in at the deep end, knowing little about company or products. Many companies don't even advise on the greeting to give, leaving it to the employee to determine what is said, depending on what they feel like at the time.

Can you imagine sending a new salesperson out on the road without a brochure, a pricelist or any other information about the company they are supposed to be selling for? It's much the same *"head in the sand"* attitude if you are simply sitting someone down in front of the telephone and expecting them to produce a great first impression when your customer calls.

### GETTING THE MESSAGE ACROSS ...

**It's a fact, unfortunately, that most lost business is due to your least well paid employee.** Think about it. You know what you want the company to look like and to feel like to the customer, and maybe, if you have a management team, they will know too. But does the office girl know, or the accounts clerk who has to cover at lunchtimes, or the part-timer who comes in to help out when you're busy, or even your wife if you happen to work from home? Do they know how you want your company image to be projected? **Do you yourself know?**

Spend just a few minutes thinking about whether or not you have a problem in this area. If you do, then make it a priority to get it sorted, because every day that you leave it to chance you are running the risk of losing potential customers who could make the difference to your bottom line.

Still on the subject of the telephone, we cannot go on without stressing the importance of answering the telephone promptly. Many companies make it a rule to answer the telephone within a certain number of rings, maybe three or four. Because some companies are leading the way and, generally, telephone answering is getting better, customers will really notice if you have a problem in this area. Ask your customers to give you their impressions. Do they have to wait too long to get their call answered, or are you right on the button? If your 'phone is ringing eight and nine times each call, you will almost certainly be losing business.

The first thing that I do when I take on work for a new company is to log the number of times the 'phone rings when I call them. I log this for a couple of weeks. I can usually tell the overall efficiency of a company from the number of rings I experience. My champion so far is a company with an average of 18 rings for every call. I stayed on the line, but I wonder how many potential customers didn't stick it out!

Once the customer has telephoned your company what happens then? Are all your staff competent enough to handle the calls in the right way?

We have already mentioned the concept that *"whatever I am doing now is the most important thing"*, and it's very important to keep that in mind when dealing with your customers on the telephone as well as when you are face to face.

**You can tell if someone on the end of the telephone isn't really taking notice of you, can't you?** There's something in their voice which gives the game away. If you're ringing to ask for some specific information about a product then you're likely to want the salesperson at the other end of the telephone to take their time with you and to go at your pace.

*But that doesn't always happen.* Maybe the salesperson is in the middle of parcelling up a package or reading through a report or even the daily newspaper! Whatever he's doing you can tell that he isn't quite giving you his full attention and that's annoying.

Just as importantly, if the salesperson is trying to get rid of the call as soon as they can, then they're going to miss some vital signs, maybe even buying signals, which may make the call very much less effective than it might have been. The message is clear, take your time over each call and cut yourself off from all other things that are going on in the office. Treat your caller as the most important person in the world and if you do and do it continuously you will see the positive results.

## PROVIDING THE RIGHT ENVIRONMENT ...

Why would a business have the problem of poor customer service on the telephone in the first place? Well, it might not be that your staff are trying to finish each call as fast as they can to get home early. It could be that they are overstretched and cannot spend as long as they would wish on each call. Whatever the reason, whether it is lack of training, insufficient guidance or some other problem, make an effort to get to the bottom of it and you'll start to ease the pressure for your staff and, at the same time, ensure that you convey a first class image to the customer too.

Other team members put pressure on colleagues taking the calls too. Do you have the type of person who stands by the desk for ages trying to get your attention while you're busy on the telephone. Invariably you have to cut a call short, only to find that what they wanted it isn't so important after all.

If you have one of these *"telephone vultures"* in your organisation, take action. Insist that no-one interrupts a colleague when they're on the telephone unless it's of the utmost importance and that no-one stands over anyone who is on the 'phone.

## GET BACK ...

Just as bad as rushing the call is not calling back. In fact I think that this is one of the most annoying things, probably because it's not only poor business practice, but downright rude too.

It's crazy, but getting called back is one of the things that impresses me most about a company. When you stop to think, it's incredible really that something we should almost take for granted should be such a major achievement. Whoever is doing the calling is actually seen as the company, so that whoever you have on the end of the telephone is either flying the company flag, or, in some cases, dragging it through the mud as they run away from the problem.

**Do you call your customers back?** Do your staff call your customers back? If you fall

*Action Point*

Be honest about how well you or your staff answer the telephone. Does everyone know what is expected of them. If not, draft out the way in which you would like to have your telephones answered. Ask your customers what they think of your telephone answering. You may be in for a shock !

*Action Point*

If you have staff, take the time to discuss call handling with them. Try to get them to understand the concept of taking time on the telephone and listen to their problems if they don't feel it is possible.

down on this one then let me tell you that you're getting yourself a reputation, and it isn't one that's creating you additional sales. Unfortunately, sometimes it isn't easy to spot that call-backs aren't being completed, especially if your business is dealing with a large number of customers. It is easier to control if you have a manageable number of key customers.

MAKING CALL BACKS MORE VISIBLE WILL ENCOURAGE THE RIGHT ATTITUDE —

If you are dealing with a manageable customer group, find out how good you are at calling them back by asking them. Ask them to compare you with your competitors too and you'll soon discover whether or not you have a problem. The chances are that if you are experiencing a problem in this area it has lost you business in the past and will do so in the future if you don't put it right.

If you do find that you have a problem, you may be able to track it down to certain individuals. They may be unable to plan their work and so never seem to have the time to call their contacts back, or it may be that they are just that type of person and view customers as problems. Either way you will want to get it sorted, either by helping them plan their day more effectively, leaving plenty of *"free"* time to complete call-backs or by reviewing whether you have the right person in the right job.

One way of getting on top of call-backs and being able to spot any lingering problems quickly is to make the function very visual and to use a large board to log the calls received which require a response. This way you can see at a glance which calls haven't been actioned and there's simply no reason for anyone to leave the office without getting back to a customer who is expecting a call. Another very important advantage of this type of system is that it will show you immediately if you have a trend of problems. You will be able to react so much quicker than if the call-backs are all in your staff's heads or on pieces of paper scattered around the office.

Call-backs are particularly important in the customer services department or, if you don't have a separate department, when you receive any type of complaint. It takes a special type of person to deal with complaints, especially if you have a continuous flow of them. If you have the right person dealing with them, you can score points over your competitors every time by a courteous and speedy reply. *If you don't have the right person on the other end of the telephone, watch out because the problems will mount.*

It's important not to view complaints as negatives. If you do, or you have staff that always feel negative when a problem crops up, then simply remind them that you're always going to get a percentage of complaints, however well you do the job. It's simply a function of being in business. Also, point out that turning a complainer into a contact who views you positively is the best way of getting a really committed customer and that this should be the aim with each and every call.

Of course, not getting back to a complainer is even more of a problem than not getting back to someone requiring information, because their problem isn't going to go away and the next time they call they'll be even more upset. A small problem can soon become a major disaster if you choose to ignore it, so try not to.

One of the best principles to keep in mind when dealing with customers demanding answers is to keep them informed at all times, even if you have nothing specific to tell them. Ringing someone just to say that *"although you have nothing further to tell them, but you haven't forgotten them"*, can earn you a considerable amount of brownie points. However, not calling can add fuel to the sometimes already out of control fire.

Suppose Mr Upset calls on Monday at 10.00am with a problem he has had over the weekend. The call is taken by the correct person in the organisation but they cannot get the information required to be able to answer the query until 2.00pm that afternoon. Our man tells Mr Upset that he'll get back to him and when Mr Upset asks if that will be today, our man says yes.

Unfortunately, what our customer services man didn't know is that the technical services manager has extended his visit to a supplier and won't return to the office until the following day. Our customer services manager waits for him to return to collect the information he needs to solve the problem. He doesn't call Mr Upset.

At 4.30pm a very angry Mr Upset telephones after staying in all afternoon waiting for a call that has never arrived and we are getting deeper and deeper into trouble.

On the other hand, what would have happened if, at 1.30pm, our man had called Mr Upset to let him know, as soon as he knew himself, that he couldn't get the information that afternoon after all because the manager wasn't returning, but that he would call tomorrow at lunchtime with the correct details. Just maybe Mr Upset would have been happy with that. Even if he wasn't totally happy, at least he would have understood more fully.

Just as when you are face to face, the important thing is to keep the customer informed, even if you have nothing to tell him. Customers always assume that they are way down a long list of other customers who are getting preferential treatment and so it is important to make sure that they realise that they haven't been forgotten and that their problem is important to you too.

In the end, people need to appreciate just how important the telephone is to the company and that each call is an opportunity to get closer to the customer, to learn more about their needs and to make the right impression. Furthermore, it's an opportunity to build a relationship and to ensure that whatever business is available in the future comes your way and doesn't disappear down the road to your competitors. *That would be sad.*

*C H A P T E R   3*
# Getting it right from start to finish

Every single time a customer or a potential customer comes into contact with your company you should be aiming to give first class service, service which stands out from the crowd and service which will get you talked about (in a nice way!).

If further information has to be sent, then make certain that it's sent quickly and that when received, the customer finds it in good condition. There's little worse than having to wait days or weeks for information you have requested and which you need urgently.

This is why the internal lead management system is so important and should be reviewed constantly to ensure that it is performing well and, more importantly, outperforming the competition. In the section covering direct mail we highlighted the elements of the pack which would make a mailing more effective. In the same way, simple information sent to a new prospect should also be viewed as an important direct mail package. Make it powerful and make it produce results.

**An effective covering letter should be written in the same way a direct mail letter would be put together.** Remember, you still only have a few seconds to grab attention, even though the customer may have requested the information. Earlier in the book I described how I had received two separate mailers on the same day and how one had caught my imagination and one hadn't. If you are sending your product details out with only a

**NOTES**

*Action Point*

Do you know how effective your information pack is? Do you know what is being sent? If you've lost contact with this important function regain control and get familiar with the package you are sending. Does it need a facelift? What is the competition sending? Do the customers think it helps them to make a decision? If you don't know, then ask them by carrying out some research with those who have received the pack recently. You may be surprised by the answers.

compliments slip attached you are missing an opportunity to sell. A good, strong letter, along with customer testimonials and a well produced leaflet will increase response significantly without costing a fortune.

As I mentioned in the action point above, you should be in touch with what your competitors are mailing. If you aren't already, get yourself on their contact lists and make sure that you request new information every few months or so. Keep an eye on how long they take to send you the information and for little clues to their progress, such as whether or not they are using a computer system. You should be able to tell this from the address label. If you keep their packs over a period of time, you will have a simple but effective profile of what seems to be working for them.

When you request information from your competitors, do so in different ways - through the post, by 'phone and by clipping a coupon if they advertise. Requesting information by telephone will give you an insight into the professionalism of their customer service and can also have another spin-off too - if you're impressed with the employee on the other end of the 'phone you can ask for their name and keep them in your *"future people"* file for when you need more staff!

Back in your own company a simple ***"Information Request Form"*** will help you to keep track of your own enquiries and improve your own lead handling. In some companies enquiries are taken on whatever scrap of paper is handy at the time. I strongly disagree with this practice for a number of reasons. Firstly, it's the easiest way to loose information - the enquiry from a major new potential customer suddenly turns up three months later on the back of the report you happened to be writing at the time. Secondly, using any old piece of paper doesn't give any sort of framework to guide whoever is taking the call.

By this I mean that there may be specific questions that you would like answers to before you send information. No matter how good you or your staff are, you will not be able to remember to ask all the questions all the time. In the majority of cases you won't ask the questions at all! Having a simple form handy will make sure that you have a better chance of securing all the important information you need - including telephone numbers and postcodes - important for database work in the future.

A simple Information Request Form could carry the following details:

Date

Person taking the details

Name and Address

Postcode

Telephone Number

How they first heard of the company

Information requested

Whether details have been sent or need to be sent

Whether or not a demonstration is required

Any other information required

Another advantage of using a standard form for lead processing is that you can round up the forms at any point in time and, in a moment, have a reasonably clear picture of what is happening regarding lead generation, always assuming that the information is being collected properly.

**Getting other people to collect the correct information when a prospect calls will be one of the hardest things you will have to do.** Somehow people just don't seem to be able to complete a form properly. You'll be frustrated that only 44% of all postcodes are collected or that most haven't been asked where they first heard about the company. Your best chance is to try to explain why it is so important that you get the information, so that you can tell if a promotion is working or are able to manage the database more effectively. At the end of the day though, you may have to count your blessings if the information is getting just a little better bit by bit.

You could even run a competition to focus on the importance of the information gathering, giving prizes for the highest percentage of correctly filled in forms, making sure, of course, that the those at the bottom of the table are mentioned too!

Not having a proper system for your lead handling can be a very serious problem, especially if you are up against competition who are good at getting the first set of details to the customer. On many occasions you could be days behind the more efficient company and your information might be landing on the doormat just as the customer is walking back through the door with the product he has already purchased, fed up of waiting for your information pack.

*The message is clear I hope.* Monitoring systems set up in your organisation, however simple, will most certainly have an impact on how the customer views you. Get them right and build them around what is best for the customer and you will win; get them wrong and put them into place for your own benefit and you will lose.

You could be spending thousands on new equipment, new product development or new promotions, but you could be throwing most of it away, merely because you haven't paid enough attention to the basics - *as I said right at the start of the book, it's very, very simple.*

## THE QUESTION IS ...

One of the most effective methods that I have found of keeping close to your customers, making them feel good, and, at the same time, acquiring lots of really useful information is by using questionnaires.

Questionnaires are an easy way of providing answers to some of the most important questions we need to know on a continuing basis such as:

**What do my customers think of my service levels?**

**Do my customers buy from my competitors?**

**Are my customers likely to buy from me again and, if so, when?**

**Which products do my customers want me to sell to them?**

These are just a few of the many questions that will provide a business with meaningful answers that can be utilised to shape future policy.

Knowing from month to month how customers view your business is a very powerful tool to have at hand. Not only do you want to be on the ball if your service levels drop for any reason, but it provides both you and your staff with a good feeling when you know for sure that you are getting it right and that your efforts are being appreciated. What's more, when you produce good results, you can use them to great effect in your sales literature to add an important confidence booster. For example:

**A recent survey has shown that over 96% of all our customers believe our service to be either excellent or very good.**

Now that's impressive stuff and details that will make more people want to do business with you. A word of warning though. If you decide to use statistics to back up your claims, make sure that they're still relevant when you use them. Don't just carry out one survey and leave it at that, make sure they are part of a programme of research so that you really do have your finger on the pulse.

There's one question which is remarkably powerful when used on a questionnaire and it's one that I would recommend using every time if appropriate. The question is:

**"If there is one thing that would make our service better, what would it be?"**

NOTES

*Action Point*

Before you decide to print an Information Request Form, photocopy your design to be used for a few weeks. Then you can make any changes you need before you incur the cost of printing. This applies to most forms.

*Quick Tip*

Ask your customers "How are we doing ?" as many times as possible. It's a very cheap way of making sure you are winning.

Using this question focuses the customer's mind and you are sure to be both surprised and interested in the replies that you receive. Your customers will give you hundreds of really good ideas, some of which you will be able to implement to make your business better almost straight away and at little cost. All the ideas you receive are free and your customers will feel involved. You can involve the customer even further by writing to them to thank them for their idea, letting them know that you really have read the questionnaire and expressing your thanks for their efforts - you may even wish to include a free gift.

Listening to the customer is really very important and if you do implement plans which concentrate on making sure that you know what your customers want, you will always be in with a chance.

## MAKING MORE OF THE QUESTIONNAIRE ...

Apart from getting very precious information about your customers and maybe generating some new ideas for the future, you can also use a questionnaire to produce valuable new sales leads too. In many cases you can design the questionnaire to do exactly that, without making it look like a sales letter. It's the final question which brings the enquiry. It can be something like:

**"Recently our company has introduced two new models of the XYZ product which you may be interested in taking a look at. If you would like further information simply tick the box."**

You can send questionnaires to all types of contacts. Customers, enquirers, suppliers - in fact anyone who you would like to have an ongoing relationship with. You can use questionnaires to find out why people didn't buy from you, why they did or if they are going to in the future. If you're creative with your questionnaires you can use them to both protect existing business and build new business too.

As with a direct mail campaign, the joy of this type of approach is that you don't have to spend too much before you know whether you are going to get a reasonable return. Sending 50 only questionnaires will give you an indication whether it is worth progressing on a grander scale. Having said that, the more you send the more you'll get back, so try to give the test a real chance by sending enough in the first place.

Treating a questionnaire as you would a direct mail package means that by sending an pre-paid or stamped envelope for the response to be returned will increase response. Including a simple offer or prize draw element will also help to increase the returns. Even remembering to send a large enough envelope, so that the customer doesn't have to fight to fold the questionnaire too many times, will all make a difference. *The customer is doing you a favour, so make it easy for them.*

Finally, on the subject of questionnaires, don't make them too long. I myself have thrown away many a questionnaire simply due to the length. I just couldn't face answering all those questions. If you need to get a lot of information, then choose a selection of questions to send and then follow up with others. Those customers who return the questionnaire are the ones who are more willing to help and so you may wish to talk to them again. You can even ask them if they would be willing to answer more questions on your original mailing.

## ONCE YOU HAVE A CUSTOMER ...

What's for sure though, is that the companies keeping in touch with their customers will always have an advantage over the ones which just wait for the customers to come back. Questionnaires are just one of the ways in which companies can show their customers that they are a little bit different from the rest, that they are the people to do business with next time. *There are many other ways too.*

Our Building Society sends our daughter a card on her birthday each year and has done since we opened an account for her. Not a particularly sophisticated marketing programme I'm sure, but one with a very high visibility level. Not only is the card seen by friends and relatives, but, when she is older the chances are that this particular Building Society will be high on the list of people to talk to about a mortgage. Maybe you too can operate a simple but effective promotion like that?

A new watch I bought recently came with an offer of a free battery whenever I needed one. It's going to get me back into the shop again, but, more than that, has kept the shop in my mind ever since I bought the watch. It won't have cost a fortune to run the promotion, but I think it's effective. In the same way, a camera shop ran a similar promotion, but went even further.

Totally out of the blue, it sent a camera battery to all customers who had bought a camera 12 months before. You and I know that when a camera battery fails you usually have to go out and get one because it isn't the type of thing you keep in the house, so this free gift would have proven very useful indeed and the shop knew that the battery would run out reasonably soon. Would they have missed out on some battery sales ? *Probably, but don't you think that the positive image it created was well worth it?*

A friend took delivery of a new car recently. On the back seat was a bunch of flowers, especially for her. She was amazed and delighted. **The car cost £12,000, the flowers £10.** She probably told more people about the flowers than the car ! When I bought a second hand car recently I received a 'phone call from the garage after six weeks, just to check that everything was all right. It was and I appreciated the call. *But shouldn't all companies be doing that too?* It cost very little, it took very little time and I was left to feel that the company actually cared about me.

## KEEPING IN TOUCH ...

Calling a customer to find out if everything is all right is such a simple thing to do, but many people don't do it because they are fearful of the reply. They think that they are going to walk into a problem. Maybe they will, but, if they do, then they should be delighted. The fact is that if the customer isn't called and has a problem, the problem isn't going to go away, it's just going to get worse!

Solving a minor problem before it becomes something more major is one of the best ways of creating a loyal customer. If you have salespeople who are looking for something useful to do in slack times, get them to call the customers who bought from them in the past few weeks - *just to check if all is well.* Calling a new customer can also be a good technique to use to generate new leads. If the existing customer is happy with their purchase and delighted that you have taken the time and the trouble to call, they may also be willing to give you the name of someone else who may be interested in the product you are selling.

Of course, if you have a product that is visible, your customer may already have had comments from friends or relations who will have indicated their desire to have one too. Simply passing on this information could produce you a constant stream of very cheap new leads.

**Becoming an excellent company to do business with is really just a matter of common sense.** If you are serious about providing great service you will already know what you would expect when you buy a product. Unfortunately, what we expect from others and what we provide ourselves can sometimes be two totally different things. Practices that we simply don't put up with when we are the customer are left to continue in our own businesses.

Maybe it's because we just haven't got the time to keep on top of everything, maybe it's because the people we are employing just don't care enough, or maybe it's because we don't take enough time or spend enough money training our people so that they actually know what we expect of them. Whatever the reason, one thing is clear: if we take the time to get the little things right we will be rewarded with increased customer satisfaction and increased business.

> *Quick Tip*
>
> Always thank the customer for their help when you send them a questionnaire and let them know why you have sent it and what you hope to achieve by it.

**NOTES**

*Action Point*

Make a note to review constantly all the aspects of your business which will impact on your customers. Look at the information packs you send out, the way the 'phones are answered, the way that complaints are dealt with. Review them every few months and aim to make them more effective. Become customer driven.

## Summary Points

1. Doing the simple things right will make sure that you stand out from the crowd.

2. If you have staff, make sure that they are aware of the standards you expect and that they are "customer orientated".

3. Don't be afraid to ask your customers what they think of your service levels. Monitor your performance at all times.

4. Get the internal information flow right.

5. Let your customers know that they are valued - as many times as possible.

# The Final Word

When I started to write this book my aim was to produce something that could be easily read, easily understood and used by a wide variety of people with little marketing experience. I hoped to provide an ongoing programme of simple marketing actions which would make a difference quickly and make the 'phones ring more often. I hope that I have achieved that in some small way.

If you have found the book useful, great; but don't just put it away, never to be seen again. If you have a *"bring forward"* file put it in there to browse through again in six months time or so. If you do I can guarantee you that you'll rediscover a number of ideas which you meant to action but didn't quite get around to.

However large your organisation becomes, never loose sight of the fact that it is the simple things that will make the biggest difference. There may be many points that you have read about which you meant to get around to months ago, or that you thought were already being actioned but that have fallen by the wayside for whatever reason. Take a good, long hard look at the little things in your business and you'll be building a stronger foundation on which to construct a winning enterprise.

**If, in 12 months time you have implemented every idea in the book, you should be pretty successful. Good luck!**

David N Russell

**P.S.** - Oh, and if you need a enthusiastic marketing professional to give you a helping hand, you know where to come!!

*Quick Tip*

Never believe that "marketing" is something that you need to be an expert at to be successful. A small amount of common sense combined with a willingness to try new ideas and keeping things simple should do the trick!!

Marketing Matters, 2 Butlin Close, Rothwell, Northants NN14 6YA. Tel. 01536 710050

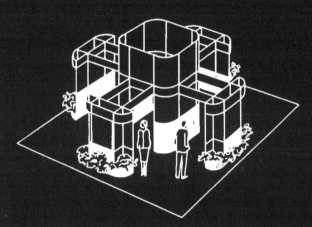
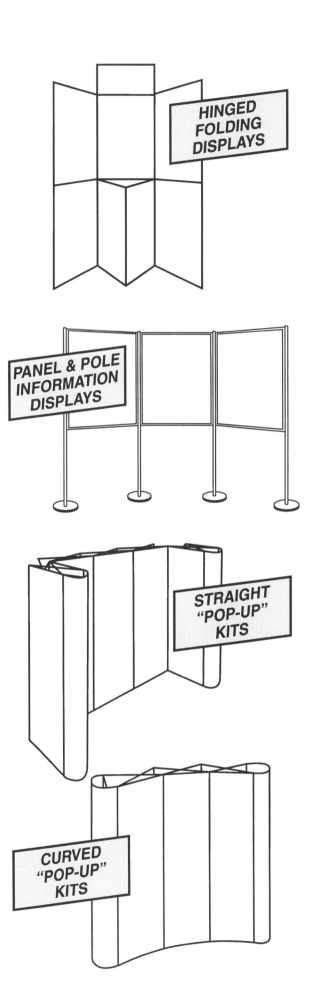